MW01118650

Reflections on Literature:
Exploring Meanings and Messages

Volume I: The Modern Novel
from the Roaring Twenties to the Mythic West

BY ROBERT VAN DELLEN, PH.D.

DORRANCE
PUBLISHING CO
EST. 1920
PITTSBURGH, PENNSYLVANIA 15238

Dorrance Publishing Co
585 Alpha Drive
Suite 103
Pittsburgh, PA 15238
Visit our website at www.dorrancebookstore.com

ISBN: 979-8-88729-278-6
eISBN 979-8-88729-778-1

Reflections on Literature:
Exploring Meanings and Messages

*Volume I: The Modern Novel
from the Roaring Twenties to the Mythic West*

Dedication

This publication and subsequent publications in this series, titled **Reflections on Literature: Exploring Meanings and Messages,** are dedicated to Sue, my wife. She has consistently encouraged and supported me from the conception of my talks on literature to the publication of these essays. Her patience, tolerance, counsel, and assistance make all this possible. She is my faithful companion and soulmate.

Table of Contents

Introduction

You are cordially invited to travel with me through space and time to enticing and engaging places, where we will meet some truly remarkable characters, experience some exciting adventures, and witness a whole array of human dynamics in action. All this is possible through the marvelous magic of literature. We will sneak a drink at a speakeasy and watch flappers dance; we will crash a party at Jay Gatsby's mansion; we will witness a bullfight in Spain; and so much more. The struggle of an old man with a giant fish, an Oakie family seeking to realize the American Dream, a cattle drive out west, and a revolution on a farm by animals—all of these are included in **Volume I** of **Reflections on Literature**.

To explain the background and context for these essays, they began as talks on literature for the Elliott Museum in Stuart, Florida, beginning in 2016 until early 2020. These were offered under the Museum's "Lectures on Literature" series, and I delivered sixteen of them, each one supported by power point slides. Then COVID hit, and the lecture series was suspended. I take this opportunity to thank the Elliott Museum for its support. However, the interest in such talks continued. I continued delivering talks on literature through Zoom, also augmented by slides. To date, I have a total of thirty presentations. The essays contained in this **Volume, The Modern Novel from the Roaring Twenties to the Mythic West**, along with the additional four volumes to follow, are the results of these talks, now presented in essay format.

I titled these five volumes, **Reflections on Literature: Exploring Mean-**

ings and Messages. They are intended to urge you to do your own reflecting about the various works and authors presented. These essays are not scholarly digs into the archeological or geological layers of any work or author discussed. On the contrary, my hope is that you, who enjoys reading and appreciates literature, will find reading these essays engaging and meaningful. Throughout all of these essays, there are some fundamental assumptions about the value and importance of literature.

In addition to the entertainment value of reading a good novel, poem, play, or short story, literature offers so much more than a mere escape. The "Meanings" and "Messages" reside, I believe, in four essential concepts, which are:

1. *Connections*. Literature unites reader and author together in an essential space of give and take that expands the reader's horizons. Not just a connection with the author, but also layers of connectivity with characters, images, settings, symbols, plots, and climaxes. Literature takes us out of our own confined reality and invites us into another one. If we are open to such expansion, the possibilities are almost endless. Of course, we make our own connections by sharing the literature with family, friends, and others.

2. *Reflections*. Literature offers us a mirror through which we are better able to understand ourselves and our world. By entering another realm through reading, we have a counterbalance to our own reality, which gives us opportunities to compare and contrast, to measure and assess, to evaluate and assimilate. What better way to gain insights than by seeing the multiple levels of reflections literature provides.

3. *Refractions*. Not only a mirror, literature also provides for us a window through which to see anew, differently, and expansively. Experiences we are not likely to ever have are offered by literature, and such experiences broaden our horizons and expand our knowledge. What a valuable resource for our intellectual and emotional growth.

4. *Enlightenment*. Literature opens doors to the possibilities of life. Thus, we are illuminated and enlightened. In a sense, literature offers us the mapping technique known as "Ground-Truthing," which allows us to verify our findings. Literature helps to center us, providing

a means for coping with reality. Through the connections, reflections, and refractions that literature gifts us, we gain wisdom about ourselves, the past, the present, and the future, as well as the complex network of human existence.

A gift that keeps on giving, all four of these concepts are thematic motifs running throughout these essays. To probe these concepts, I consciously wander rather far and wide over a diverse range of topics from the classical writings of William Shakespeare and William Blake to a contemporary novel by Miranda Cowley Heller, **The Paper Palace**. We will look at the poetry of T. S. Eliot, Maya Angelou, and Mary Oliver, as well as the great Walt Whitman and Robert Frost.

The intensity of great drama and journeys into the realms of friendships, loves, and facing our end of life are also provided. I arrange these essays around genres or themes. **Volume I, The Modern Novel from the Roaring Twenties to the Mythic West**, begins with the eclectic and chaotic period in our history known as the "Roaring Twenties." Often referred to as the "Lost Generation," we will look at the historical context that gave us jazz and motion pictures on the one hand while prohibiting liquor. From Langston Hughes and Bessie Smith to Ernest Hemingway and F. Scott Fitzgerald, this amazing time frame produced a virtual explosion in dance, music, the arts, and literature. I follow the discussion of this period with a close look at Hemingway's **The Old Man and the Sea**, which I believe is his finest work.

We then explore the life and works of John Steinbeck, truly an American icon. My essay on the American West and its writers discusses the mythic dimensions of the West and the need to demythologize when such myths do great damage. One glaring example of such damage is the stereotyping of Native Americans. I conclude **Volume I** with a close look at two of the best works of fiction by George Orwell, **Animal Farm** and **1984**. We face divisive, contentious, and troubling times today in which the politics of power all too often recede into policies of exploitation, discrimination, and fake news. Orwell remains both prophetic and prescient today. His voice is still disturbingly relevant and his warnings are very alarming.

Provided **Volume I** enjoys sufficient readers to justify publishing **Volume II**, the plan is to come out with the following four volumes is succession, one shortly following the previous one. **Volume II, Touching Our Souls: The Significance of Poetry,** seeks to illustrate that poetry is worthwhile for all of us, even those who have a built-in resistance or barrier standing in the way of appreciation. After all, poetry is about making connections, holding up mirrors, and providing windows as passageways to our enlightenment and enjoyment. We will experience the magnetic messages of the great Maya Angelou, who sings to free her and our souls. Mary Oliver, one of my favorite poets, connects us to the wonders of nature with flights of geese and messages of hope. Any discussion of American poetry should include Walt Whitman and Robert Frost, two very different voices that inspire reverence and reflection. I will also explore the challenging, complicated, and complex William Blake as a painter and a poet, arguing that he, too, has a prophetic voice that is still relevant. I end **Volume II** sharing a whole range of different poems and poets, with the hopes that I open doors and invite you inside the magic, mystery, and majesty of poetry.

Volume III, Dramatic Encounters: Four Great Playwrights, explores the theatrical brilliance of Eugene O'Neill, Tennessee Williams, Arthur Miller, and William Shakespeare. We will examine in some detail specific plays by each of these master dramatists. My discussion of Shakespeare explains his contrasting vision of both the tragic and the comic world order. They form a dialectical tension that invites us to laugh at ourselves but also to see the dark night of the human soul.

Life's Lessons from Literature: Friendship, Love, Death; Huck Finn, King Lear, Moby Dick, Thoreau, and Others is a diverse collection of essays in **Volume IV.** We will explore what literature teaches us about growing up and growing old, about friendships and loves, about realized and rejected relationships, about complicated family dynamics. To learn these lessons, we will return to poetry, classical works, contemporary novels, and some of the standard greats. This volume ends with the urgency of Henry David Thoreau, perhaps our first environmentalist, who beckons us to protect our fragile earth.

Literature invites us on a journey—a journey of discovery. It offers us roadmaps into new territories. **Volume V** is titled **Literary Wanderings: Journeys and Destinations from Impressionism to Pat Conroy and Louise Penny.** We will look at a vast array of literature that deals with Impressionist art. We will explore some of our very best nature writers and look closely at some of their "Odes to Earth." We will enter the agonized but so very human world of Pat Conroy, whose novels so eloquently portray both the angst and the wonder of life. We end with the marvelous world of Louise Penny and her cast of delightful characters. While murder is the central drama of her enticing plots, we are always left with a smile of hope, a glimmer of optimism, a faith that life is indeed worth living.

This gives you a sketch of my five volumes. The essays are meant to probe, prod, provoke, and process a diverse range of some of the very best literature from England and the United States. I hope they give you worthwhile "Meanings" and "Messages." I hope our journey together makes connections, evokes reflections, invites refractions, and enlightens and delights. Thank you for your support and interest. You make all this possible, and for that I am very grateful.

Robert Van Dellen
February, 2023

Notice of Intent

As I explained, these essays were first prepared and presented as talks, complete with power point slides. Like the talks, these essays are intended for the edification of a general audience— people who love to read and benefit from it. They are consciously not in accordance with traditional academic protocol, with footnotes, bibliographies, and sources cited. The contents contained herein are begged, borrowed, cut, and pasted from a variety of sources, most of which are readily available on the internet, such as Wikipedia and other resources. Most of the biographical information about an author can be found in any number of sources. The interpretations of a particular work by an author are primarily my own. Where this interpretation was especially influenced by a particular source, I have tried to give credit. I am well aware that my interpretations are subject to differing interpretations. Any errors of facts presented in these essays are my own, and I take responsibility for them.

SEARCHING FOR THE LOST GENERATION:
Literature During The Roaring Twenties

As a lifelong student and former professor of literature, the 1920s is one of my favorite periods. It produced some of the very best plays, novels, short stories, and poetry in all of Western Civilization, along with outstanding art, music, and dance. Many classics from this period stand tall on the world stage of great literature. It was a time when the arts exploded in the United States, France, England, and post-war Germany. Places such as Chicago, New York, Sydney, Paris, Toronto, London, and Los Angeles were hotbeds of creative productions. The decade of the 1920s was called the "crazy years," "the Jazz Age," the "Lost Generation," and the "Roarin' Twenties."

Societies throughout the world, especially the Western World, were going through rapid, dramatic, seismic transformations. The world had tilted, paradigms had shifted, and there was no returning to the way things used to be, despite some notable efforts to stop this speeding train of change. The decade roared with intensity that still captures our imagination over a hundred years later. I will be exploring some of the very best literature that came out of this period. It is too vast to cover all of it, so this is a representational sampling, with the hopes that it will encourage you to do additional searching on your own.

I begin with two great poets and some lines from two of their very best poems. They set the stage, for they are indicative of the times. They capture the themes we will see repeatedly presented in the literature of this period.

Listen to the opening lines of "The Second Coming," by William Butler Yeats (1919):

> Turning and turning in the widening gyre
> The falcon cannot hear the falconer;
> Things fall apart; the centre cannot hold;
> Mere anarchy is loosed upon the world....

The poem begins with a sense of things spinning out of control. There is a nightmare tone to it all. The poem captures a profound sense of loss and anxiety. The imagery throughout the poem is violent, terrifying. Yeats describes the second coming as a rough beast in direct contrast to a gentle Jesus, a beast emerging from the desert and slouching toward Bethlehem. There is clearly a sense of doom and gloom, even apocalyptic.

Unfortunately, this sense of chaos and lost innocence is played out again and again in the literature of the period. It is important to explore why. Two important questions to ponder: First, why did this period produce such an abundance of outstanding literature? Second, why does all this bleak and dismal literature, with often such depressing and painful story lines, still resonate with us over 100 years later?

Here are the opening lines from T. S. Eliot's "The Waste Land" (1922):

> April is the cruellest month, breeding
> Lilacs out of the dead land, mixing
> Memory and desire, stirring
> Dull roots with spring rain.

April, the month when Easter usually occurs, is depicted as a month that is merciless, causing pain, in a land that is wasted, barren, empty. This poem also has an apocalyptic tone to it, suggesting that innocence is truly lost, the old values and norms no longer apply, and we are entering a world unlike we have ever known.

In an effort to understand better that world and from where such disquieting voices came, it is important to put this decade in a larger historical context. What were some of the political, social, cultural, and economic factors of the 1920s that provide the background for these creative outbursts in literature? Here are some of the highlights as brief bullet points, realizing that each of these deserve far more attention than provided here:

> *WWI Ended in 1918*. With the end, there was an explosion of pent-up frustrations, a need to celebrate, and a rush to embrace newfound freedoms.

> *Art Is One Illustration of a New Reality*. There was an outburst of interest in art deco, and expressionism, and surrealism took art beyond impressionism.

> *Photography Comes Into Its Own*. Dorothea Lange, Ansel Adams, Alfred Stieglitz, and others show us new ways of seeing.

> *Feminism, Fashion, and Freedom*. Coco Chanel, flapper craze, and women gained the right to vote in 1920. The Equal Rights Amendment was passed in 1923.

> *A Newfound Hedonism*. It was fun, frantic, frenetic, and frenzied.

> *The Harlem Renaissance*. Jazz, literature, dance, the blues also exploded with the likes of Langston Hughes, Billie Holliday, Bessie Smith, Duke Ellington, and Louis Armstrong, to mention a few.

> *Homosexuality Comes Out of the Closet*. Mae West's **The Drag** was performed in 1927 to sold-out crowds.

> *The Birth of Psychoanalysis*. Sigmund Freud, Alfred Adler, Carl Jung, among others, taught us about the ego and the id, the importance of dreams, and raised awareness about depression and mental illness.

> *Mass Production, Consumerism, Economic Boom, Urbanization, and the Automobile All Brought About Major Changes in the Social, Political, and Cultural Live of Many in the US and Europe*. By 1927, when Ford Motor Company discontinued the popular Model T, over 15 million had been sold. By 1929, there were approximately 27 million vehicles traveling US streets and roads. Also in 1927, Charles Lindbergh flew the first solo, nonstop, transatlantic flight, which took 33½ hours. By the end of the 1920s, over half of all Americans lived in cities. The US economy was growing at an unprecedented pace.

> *The Radio and the Emergence of Movies and Movie Theaters Gave Birth to Mass Media, Mass Entertainment, and Mass Marketing*. Popular culture

was born with the creation of mass media. Families gathered around the radio to listen to favorite shows. In 1926, **Don Juan** was a smash hit at the rapidly growing movie houses. It was a feature-length production that included music and other sound effects. One year later, **The Jazz Singer**, starring Al Jolson, was a huge success. Warner Brothers Studio and Walt Disney Animation Studio all arose during this time.

> *Professional and College Sports also Exploded.* Babe Ruth, Jack Dempsey, Red Granger, Knute Rockne, the Harlem Globetrotters, Man O' War, Bobby Jones and others became very well-known, popular figures during this era.

> *Politics.* Warren Harding ran for president using the slogan "America First," and spent a whopping $8 Million on his campaign. Harding's administration was seen as one of the most corrupt in US history, fraught with major scandals, such as the Teapot Dome affair. After Harding's sudden death in 1923, Calvin Coolidge became president. His inauguration speech was the first to be carried on the radio. He was followed by Herbert Hoover, who was elected in 1928.

> *Significant Counter Movements: Fundamentalism, Prohibition, KKK, and the Mob.* The evangelical Protestant Churches gained a loud and judgmental voice during this era. By the mid-1920s, a significant number of states passed laws prohibiting the teaching of evolution in public high schools and colleges.

Remember the famous "Monkey Trail," where the pugnacious Clarence Darrow defended John Scopes in Tennessee for teaching evolution. The lead prosecutor was William Jennings Bryan, who was retained by the World Christian Fundamentalist Union. John Scopes was found guilty and fined $100.00. Of course, these same fundamentalists supported Prohibition, which was passed at the end of the war and lasted until 1933.

Another loud voice during this period was the rapid growth of the Ku Klux Klan. By the mid-1920s, it had a membership of around 4 million people and was aggressively recruiting children. Several key political seats were filled by Klan members.

Of course, Prohibition gave birth to the popular speakeasies in the US, which became very chic during this time. And the other notable development was the emergence of the mob. Remember the movie, **The Untouchables**, starring Robert De Niro and Kevin Costner. It also became a popular TV show. Despite the obvious widespread corruption caused by organized crime, there had been and remains a certain romanticized fascination and attraction. Like sex, crime sells.

> *The War & Pandemic.* WWI caused the death of approximately 22 million civilians and soldiers with another 20 million wounded. The Spanish Flu, which began in 1918 and ended in 1920, infected 500 million people worldwide, about one third of the world's population at the time. This pandemic took the lives of an estimated 25 million people, with some claiming the real number could be as high as 100 million. With these two back-to-back horrible and deadly events impacting the world, it is easy to understand that the Roarin' Twenties was eager to break out and dance the night away.

One of the interesting points to understand is that the war did play a major role in much of the literature of the period. It is often there as a shaping factor, a voice, a presence, a haunting reality. **All Quiet on the Western Front**, published in 1929, was very popular, telling the story of a German soldier's physical and mental stress during the war and his difficult adjustment to civilian life after the war. In contrast, the Spanish Flu is not very present in the literature. It is mentioned here and there, and there may be a character infected by it, but it basically remains

> *The Roar Ceased.* The decade ended with the financial crash on October 29, 1929, which became known as Black Tuesday. *Puff?!* The era ended and the Great Depression began.

There are many good historical studies of this period, as well as some excellent historical novels set during the 1920s, Two excellent books about this period and its writers are: **A Second Flowering: Works and Days of the Lost Generation** (1973) and **Exile's Return: A Literary Odyssey of the 1920s** (1951) both by Malcolm Cowley. If you want to get a taste for the period, smell the smells, experience the wild and crazy parties, and gain insights into the complexities of some of the key players, I recommend the following four books, recognizing there are many others to suggest as well.

First and foremost, Hemingway's **A Moveable Feast** (1964) stands as one of the best. As an autobiographical memoir, he began writing it while living in Cuba in 1957, but he didn't finish it until the spring of 1960. Mary, his fourth wife, edited the manuscript and had it published in 1964, three years after his death. He lived in Paris from 1921–1928 with his first wife, except for the last year, which was when he was with his second wife, Pauline. He actually found the notes he had made for the book while in Paris. They were in a trunk stored in a Paris hotel, which Hemingway returned to years later.

This memoir is a series of sketches or vignettes about people and places in Paris, some very flattering and some not very flattering. The epigraph to the book reads: "If you are lucky enough to have lived in Paris as a young man, then wherever you go for the rest of your life, it stays with you, for Paris is a movable feast." There are twenty of these sketches, covering such topics as his favorite café; his mentor, Gertrude Stein, with whom he has a love-hate relationship; the famous Shakespeare and Company Bookstore; several about his fellow writers, with which he also had admiration at times and jealous criticism at others, such as Ford Madox Ford, Ezra Pound, and F. Scott Fitzgerald. He is also unkind in the book to F. Scott's wife, Zelda.

Of course, F. Scott Fitzgerald's two novels about this era are classics. **The Beautiful and Damned**, published in 1922, portrays the New York café society and the Eastern elite right after the end of WWI and in the heat, literally, of the Jazz Age. The main characters are complex, open studies for psychoanalysis. They are driven by materialism, greed, and jealousy. Very autobiographical, the lead character is a New York socialite and heir to his tycoon father's fortune. His complicated and difficult marriage to Gloria exposes their life of heavy drinking and partying, packed with bitter, selfish pettiness and bickering. This morality tale of modern lives on the dung heap of destructiveness reveals the emptiness of a post-war world among the rich.

Three years later, Fitzgerald published what still stands as one of the greatest American novels, as well as in the entire world of fiction, **The Great Gatsby**. Living in the fictional towns of West Egg and East Egg on prosperous Long Island in the summer of 1922, the novel depicts the famous parties at the estate of Jay Gatsby. Jay, a young and mysterious millionaire, has a passionate obsession with the beautiful Daisy Buchanan. The novel is narrated by Nick Carraway, a Yale graduate from the Midwest and a veteran of the war. Daisy and Nick are cousins. Daisy is married to Tom Buchanan, a former football star at Yale, whom Nick knew during their college days. At one of the Gatsby parties, Nick meets Jordan Baker, a champion golfer and partygoer, who knew Daisy as a child. Nick and Jordan have a romantic relationship. Jordan informs Nick that Tom, Daisy's husband, is having an affair with Myrtle Wilson. The messy lives of these characters unfolds with bitter brashness and brilliant writing by Fitzgerald.

As the summer progresses and the parties at Gatsby's gothic mansion get more and more wild, we learn that Gatsby has been in love with Daisy for years and that he spends many nights staring at the green light as the end of her dock, across the bay. Nick arranges a meeting between Gatsby and Daisy and they rekindle their love and have an affair. Tom discovers this affair and is outraged by it, even though he himself is having an affair with Myrtle. Tom reveals that Gatsby made his fortune as a bootlegger and other criminal activities. Daisy accidently hits and kills Myrtle while driving Gatsby's car. Tom tells George, Myrtle's husband, that it was Gatsby who killed his wife. In a fit of rage, George goes to Gatsby's estate and shoots him while he is in his pool and then shoots himself. Nick has a small funeral for Gatsby, ends his empty affair with Jordan, and reflects on the corruption of wealth and the emptiness of the American Dream. This classic novel has been made into five movies, with the first in 1926 and the most recent in 2013 starring Leonardo DiCaprio as Jay Gatsby.

The fourth book that captures these times is Hemingway's **The Sun Also Rises**, published in 1926. The novel portrays American and British expatriates living in Paris, seeking fame and fortune as writers or artists, their intertwined lives and their preoccupation with the running of the bulls and bullfights in Spain. Highly autobiographical, many Hemingway scholars consider this his best novel. With vivid descriptions of the sordid café life in Paris and the empty relationships that seek excitement via fishing trips and bullfights, Hemingway captures the sense of a "Lost Generation" and its decadence. The novel has some of the best descriptions of bullfighting in literature. A movie was made of the novel in 1957 starring Tyrone Power as Jake Barnes, the disillusioned and wounded journalist living in Paris after the war, struggling with his masculinity. Ava Gardner and Errol Flynn also starred in this movie. Another movie came out in 1984, with Jane Seymour and Leonard Nimoy. One of the two epigraphs to the novel comes from the Book of Ecclesiastes, which reads in part: "The sun also ariseth, and the sun goeth down...." The other epigraph comes from Gertrude Stein and reads: "You are all a lost generation."

A contemporary book that eloquently captures the flavor of Paris during this time period is the beautifully written historical novel by Paula McLain, **The Paris Wife**, published in 2011. We get to know Hemingway intimately, with all his quirks and insecurities. We also get to know his first wife, Hadley Richardson, her deep love for him, and we meet Gertrude Stein, Ezra Pound, Fitzgerald, and others. Here is one passage from this fine novel that gives you a sense of both the book and the times. Hadley Richardson is being escorted home by a friend, named Don Stewart, after leaving a crowded café table with a woman fawning over Ernest, which he encourages in front of their friends. Paula McLain has Don Stewart say: "I want things to make sense again. They haven't in a long time."

To which Hadley replies: "I believed I'd understood him at the time, but now as Don walked me back to the hotel, I felt our connection more strongly. I wanted things to make sense, too. More than anything."

The novel ends with Ernest having a public affair with Pauline Pfeifer, who would become his second wife. The novelist suggests, and I think she is correct, that if Hemingway could have gotten away with keeping Hadley, with whom he had a child, as his wife and also marry Pauline, he would have preferred that. Of course, neither Hadley nor Pauline would allow that kind of an arrangement, and the law would not either.

Another excellent historical novel that takes place during the 1920s is Mary Doria Russell's marvelous coming of age story, entitled **Dreamers of the Day**, published in 2008. This novel is mainly set in the Middle East, with such actual characters as the young Winston Churchill and T. E. Lawrence, better known as Lawrence of Arabia. The novel creatively blends the personal story of a woman breaking out of her protective and emotionally paralyzing Puritanical straightjacket from her conservative upbringing in Ohio, reinforced by her manipulative mother and the political postwar machinations that created today's Middle East mess. The harsh reality of the Spanish Flu pandemic does play a major role in this novel, especially in the beginning, where people are dying frequently and suddenly.

The novel ends with a fascinating debate about dreams and dreamers, and quotes lines from T. E. Lawrence, where he maintains that: "All men dream but not equally. Those who dream by night wake in the day to find that it was vanity; but the dreamers of the day are dangerous men, for they may act their dream with open eyes to make it possible."

The novel raises this important question: *Can you predict the future by knowing the past?*

In other words, what is the value of studying history, of reading literature, of appreciating art and music? Beyond entertainment, is it perhaps so that we do not repeat past mistakes, commit the same destructive acts, and diminish rather than enhance the human condition? These are, after all, the questions the Lost Generation writers explore.

Who are some of the other important writers of the period and what is lost about them? The list is extensive. We cannot possibly examine all of them, but let us explore some of them to illustrate their basic themes, what they say to us, why they matter, and how to find our way through their dark despair to land in a brighter place?

In addition to Fitzgerald and Hemingway, there are well over thirty (30) writers of varying degrees of fame and success included in a list of members of the Lost Generation. Here are some of the names in no particular order: T. S. Eliot, William Butler Yeats, Ezra Pound, Archibald MacLeish, Hart Crane, E. E. Cummings, Sherwood Anderson, John Dos Passos, John Steinbeck, William Faulkner, Thomas Wolfe, Edna St. Vincent Millay, Henry Miller, James Joyce, D. H. Lawrence, Aldous Huxley, Jean Paul Sartre, Simone de Beauvoir, Dashiell Hammett, Virginia Woolf, J. R. R. Tolkien, Sinclair Lewis, Upton Sinclair, and Ford Madox Ford. I have probably overlooked some that should be on this list. You, no doubt, recognize most of these names and perhaps have read many of their works.

To give you some idea of the magnitude of the creative outpouring during the 1920s, here is a partial list of some of the very best novels of the period. Again, this is a representative sampling. There were well over 500 noteworthy novels published in the major Western countries during this era. The following are well worth reading or rereading. They give us an excellent sense of this time frame.

> D. H. Lawrence, **Women in Love**, 1920. Made into a movie in 1969, starring Glenda Jackson, the novel follows the loves and lives of two sisters, one of whom is an artist and in a very destructive relationship with a man while the other sister, a teacher, has a romantic friendship with a cynical intellectual. Set in pre-WWI British society and its crass class and economic conditions, the novel examines the emotional relationships of the four main characters and their psychological tensions in the context of a very confining society.

> Edith Wharton, **The Age of Innocence**, 1920. This is Wharton's twelfth novel and one of her best, earning her a Pulitzer Prize. The novel is set in the 1870s among the upper class in New York City, at a time known as "The Gilded Age." It dramatically exposes that innocence is anything but innocent.

> Sinclair Lewis, **Main Street**, 1920. This highly satirical novel set in Main Street in a town in Minnesota, where the main character comes in conflict with the small-town mentality of the residents and their refusal to consider other ways of doing and seeing things. The novel won Lewis the Nobel Prize.

> James Joyce, **Ulysses**, 1922. This massive novel develops the "stream-of-consciousness" style of writing as we witness the psychological, intellectual, and emotional ups and downs of Leopold Bloom in Dublin in the course of one ordinary day, June 16, 1904. The novel draws a number of parallels between Bloom's life and the epic poem, **The Odyssey**. It sets the stage for what comes to be called Modern Literature.

> E. M. Forster, **A Passage to India**, 1924. This is one of the very best novels about British colonialism and the exploitation by Britain of India—its resources, culture, and people. Along with George Orwell's **Burmese Days**, published ten years after this novel, both novels depict the reality of this statement by Orwell: "When the white man turns tyrant, it is his own freedom that he destroys" (from the short story "Shooting an Elephant").

> Theodore Dreiser, **An American Tragedy**, 1925. This is a big read, a massive book, based on a famous murder in 1906 and the trial. This novel weaves a complicated and involved plot and cast of characters

taking you through high drama and the lost innocence of the American Dream. This is a novel well worth reading.

> Virginia Woolf, **Mrs. Dalloway**, 1925. One of Woolf's best novels, it details the day in the life of Clarissa Dalloway, a high-society woman in post-WWI England as she makes detailed and meticulous preparations for a party she is hosting that evening. Traveling back and forth in time and to various places, the novel gives you keen insight into upper-class London life and the hollowness of it all in the aftermath of the war and its impact on England.

> Thomas Wolfe, **Look Homeward Angel**, 1929. One of my very favorite novels, this is the story of the "Buried Life" at the end of the era. It is highly autobiographical, telling the story of the coming of age of Eugene Gant from his birth in 1900 to the time he leaves home at the age of nineteen. Set in a fictional town in North Carolina, the novel gives us an in-depth look at family life, the struggles of a young boy with an alcoholic father, tragic deaths, and economic failure. Alienated and out of place, Gant's struggles to adjust, his obsessions with a woman, and his fight to carve out a place for himself are powerfully depicted in the novel.

> William Faulkner, **The Sound and the Fury**, 1929. Also using the "stream-of-consciousness" writing style, Faulkner's classic novel, his fourth, is set in Jefferson, Mississippi and centers around the Compson family. This gothic novel describes the former Southern aristocrats who now struggle with the dissolution of their family and its reputation. The family has fallen into financial ruin, lost its religious faith, and is no longer respected. A difficult read because of its complicated narrative shifts, this is truly a great novel and deserves to be read or re-read.

A. A. Milne's **Winnie-the-Pooh** and Kahlil Gibran's **The Prophet** were also written and published during this time. Also, Adolf Hitler published his famous **Mein Kampf**, in 1925. Written while he was in prison, the work describes his passionate hatred of Jews and his equally passionate white supremacist concepts about the superiority of the Germans.

This representative list does not include plays, short stories, or poetry that were also produced during this highly creative time. Perhaps our greatest playwright, Eugene O'Neill, wrote **Anna Christie, Desire Under the Elms,** and **Strange Interlude** during this period. The term "Lost Generation" is attributed by Hemingway to Gertrude Stein. In the aftermath of the war, these young artists were profoundly impacted by the war, some were wounded, and most knew people killed. There was an overall mood of emptiness. The world made no sense. Remember the Yeats poem about the center not holding. Disillusionment was the main meal of the day. Most of these writers were then in their twenties or early thirties. Many lost faith in traditional values and were cynical about leadership and patriotism. There was a malaise, a recklessness, and a dark gloom hanging over all the drinking and dancing.

The literature they created during this time carried the familiar and dominant theme of decadence. Consider the lavish parties in Fitzgerald's **The Great Gatsby** or the aimless traveling, drinking, and parties in **The Sun Also Rises.** These works expose the sordid nature of shallow, frivolous lives. Despite all the parties, there is an underlying sense of loneliness, isolation, alienation—a helplessness, powerlessness, and impotence. In **The Sun Also Rises,** Jake is literally impotent as a result of a war wound. Hemingway himself suffered a war wound. These writers shattered idealized dreams and exposed disillusionment. These famous closing lines from **The Great Gatsby** capture the malaise: "Gatsby believed in the green light, the orgastic future that year by year recedes before us. It eluded us then, but that's no matter—tomorrow we will run faster, stretch our arms farther.... And one fine morning—So we beat on, boats against the current, borne back ceaselessly into the past."

Many of these artists expatriated to Paris where they lived and worked for extended periods of time. Paris was the Mecca. It was recovering rapidly from the war, the economy was booming, and you could live relatively cheaply there. And you could drink legally. The cafés were crowded with painters, writers, and groupies. Some of the most famous writers of the period who lived in Paris for part of the time were: John Dos Passos, Ford Madox Ford, Ezra Pound, Hemingway, Fitzgerald, Henry Miller, and James Joyce. They all met, partied, and discussed their works while in Paris. And they were often joined by the French writers Jean Paul Sartre, his companion Simone de Beauvoir, Andre Gide, and others. They shared their works, met in cafés and at Gertrude Stein's salon and the Shakespeare and Company bookstore to discuss literary theories and modernism as a movement.

At the center of all this, was the "Grande Dame" of the arts in Paris during this time, Gertrude Stein (1874–1946—72). A novelist, poet, playwright, and art collector, as well as a mentor in Paris to many aspiring writers, Gertrude was born in Pittsburgh and was raised in Oakland, California. Her parents came from upper-middle-class, Jewish families, and her father was a wealthy businessman with extensive real estate holdings. She grew up with both English and German spoken in their home. When she was three years old, her family moved to Vienna and then to Paris, teaching the Stein children a deep affection for culture, art, and literature.

Gertrude was raised in the Jewish faith and traditions. She attended Radcliffe College and studied under the famous psychologist William James. She struggled often with depression. In 1902, she traveled with her brother Leo to London and the next year to Paris, where she lived the rest of her life.

From 1903–1914, Gertrude and Leo shared living quarters on the Left Bank of Paris and began the serious business of collecting art. In fact, they managed to acquire a substantial collection of emerging artists, such as several works by Henri Matisse, Cezanne, Renoir, Gauguin, and early Picassos. Their collection eventually grew to be worth a fortune. Their living quarters also served as a gallery and salon that numerous artists visited frequently. When brother and sister eventually split up, Leo moved to Florence. Although they split their holdings, Gertrude remained a very wealthy woman. When times became rough for her, especially as a Jew living in Paris when WWII broke out, she would sell off some paintings in order to maintain her lifestyle. Gertrude and Leo had a falling out and did not speak for thirty years. There is strong evidence that she was able to survive in German-occupied Paris during the war because of friendships she developed with Nazi-supported government officials who were puppets of the Hitler regime.

As important as her art collection was for her, the mentoring of aspiring writers who had gathered in Paris was also highly valued by her. In 1907, Gertrude met Alice B. Toklas on the very day Alice arrived in Paris. They immediately became intimate friends and lifelong companions. Alice moved in to live with Gertrude. Together they managed a lively salon from their home. Stein was open, gracious, willing to give advice, and used her influence to contact editors and publishers. She also occasionally lent money to the struggling artists. The power of her influence was substantial.

Although her published works have not survived her reputation, she was well respected as a writer during her life. She produced a rather impressive list of publications, including short stories, novels, essays, and plays. Her 1933 autobiographical memoir, **The Autobiography of Alice B. Toklas**, was a bestseller and was widely discussed, as well as her other works that dealt openly and unapologetically with homosexuality. She is credited with helping to develop a stream-of-consciousness style, which was so effectively used by James Joyce.

In October of 1934 and lasting for six months, Gertrude returned to the US and embarked on a lecture tour that took her to thirty-seven cities and twenty-three states. These were enormously popular and well attended. She returned to France in May of 1935 having successfully landed a publishing contract with Random House, who committed to publishing all of her new works. Upon her return to Paris, the **Chicago Daily Tribune** wrote: "No writer in years has been so widely discussed, so much caricatured, so passionately championed."

To be sure, Gertrude was a very controversial character, but she was also very influential. She supported gay rights, feminism, immigration, and she played major roles in encouraging writers and painters. Yet she also endorsed Franco during the Spanish Civil War and collaborated with Nazis in Paris during WWII, perhaps for her own survival. She died on July 27, 1946 after surgery for stomach cancer at the American Hospital in France, and she is buried at the famous Père Lachaise Cemetery in Paris. Alice B. Toklas died later and is buried next to Gertrude. If you go to Paris, visiting this cemetery should be on your "Must Do" list. You can stand at the gravesites of Jim Morrison, Chopin, Oscar Wilde, Edith Piaf, Balzac, and many other famous people.

Although Gertrude Stein's writings are now, for the most part, ignored, save for some graduate students studying twentieth century literature, she remains an important and influential character in the drama of the Roarin' Twenties. She brought artists and writers together, gave them space, mentored them, and in several cases helped them get published and public recognition. Despite the falling out between her and Hemingway and the cruel things Hemingway said about her in **A Moveable Feast**, Gertrude Stein deserves respect and appreciation. She played an important role in Paris during this period.

There are so many other worthwhile writers to consider. The great poet, Edna St. Vincent Millay, who was in Paris for a time, and who was awarded the Pulitzer Prize for poetry in 1923. Her life and works stand tall among the giants we have discussed. The great Virginia Woolf wrote and published **Mrs. Dalloway**, **To The Lighthouse**, and **Orlando** during the 1920s. For these two women authors to gain recognition was enormous, for writing was still predominantly a man's realm. I touched briefly on **Main Street** by Sinclair Lewis, but he also wrote and published three other noteworthy novels during this era: **Babbitt**, a powerful satire of American commercialism; **Arrowsmith**, which earned him a Pulitzer Prize and describes the challenges an idealistic doctor faces; and **Elmer Gantry**, which exposes the self-righteous hypocrisy of a Bible-thumping, evangelical minister. You may have seen the 1960 movie starring Burt Lancaster, who received the Best Actor Oscar for his performance. There is certainly no shortage of excellent novels, plays, poems, and short stories well worth knowing from this period.

In conclusion, the war left our writers feeling alienated and with a lost and acute sense of disillusionment. Their literature depicts these. There was a pervasive angst, what the philosopher Kierkegaard called the "Dark Night of the Soul." These writers formed an extensive network of support, which generated a strong synergy. They discussed modernism, shared their works, and they encouraged one another.

There was a kind of Community of Comrades, very similar to the Impressionist painters in France at the end of the nineteenth century. They competed to be sure, but they also fed off each other. Feeling this deep sense of being lost, they found strength and creative capacity as part of this club of writers. There was a great deal of cross-fertilization among them. Gertrude Stein's support clearly stimulated a significant part of this creative productivity.

Eugene O'Neill stated this about tragedy: "To me, the tragic alone has that significant beauty which is truth. It is the meaning of life—and the hope." This enormously impressive collection of outstanding works deals with the fragileness of the human condition and the whole range of complex human conditions. As O'Neill asserted, the very act of exposing all this implies hope. Amidst all the gloom and doom, all the darkness and hollowness, there burns a bright light at the end of the dock. The underlying statement beneath it all is that we have resilience, we have an untapped capacity to overcome, we have a spirit of survival, and we have unrealized possibilities waiting to happen. The literature of the Roaring Twenties challenges us to elevate ourselves. It invites us into the powerful truths of these creative imaginations. Beyond the darkness, the sense of loss, and the void of emptiness, there is a deep reservoir of compassion, understanding, and kindness.

In addition to the sheer genius on display by the literature of this period, along with the mastery of craft, the incredibly well-written stories, and the memorable characters, this literature, like all great art, transcends the very place and time in which it is set. It transforms us into another space and connects us to our human family, implicitly begging for that family to be kinder and gentler. It calls us to have a truer moral compass and to see ourselves beyond our own limited sense of time and place as part of the larger human community. Great literature chronicles what it means to be human. It exposes the absolutes in life, the very foundations of human existence. The fundamentals of life are the subject matter of literature. It opens wide the doors of understanding the complexities of these emotions.

If we allow ourselves to be open to the experiences of these writings, there is something magical and mysterious about them. There is pleasure in reading well-tuned words, like the notes of a blues song. We meet fascinating people and are cascaded down the rapids of an engaging story. In the final analysis, all great art offers us both a window and a mirror. The window opens whole new vistas and horizons. The mirror reflects our own souls and prods us to a deeper understanding of who we are and the world in which we live.

We connect to great literature because we have tasted pain, suffered hardships, seen loss, and experienced so much of the very stuff about which it is crafted. It echoes in the chambers of our hearts and souls. We have a sense of having been there or known it. There is a strong line of connectivity. The writer knows that, knows that there is a symbiotic relationship between reader and author. Otherwise, why bother to write and why bother to read? While showing us the darkness, they show us importantly the contrasting light. These writers understand that hope grows from knowledge. While they give us the richness and nuance of shadows, they also radiate the brightness of human existence. What gifts they give us.

SEARCHING FOR THE LOST GENERATION:
LITERATURE DURING THE ROARING TWENTIES

Authors & Works Cited As Presented

William Butler Yeats, "The Second Coming," 1920

T.S. Eliot, The Waste Land, 1922

Mae West, The Drag, 1927

Erich Maria Remarque, All Quiet on the Western Front, 1929

Malcolm Cowley, A Second Flowering: Works and Days of the Lost Generation, 1973

Exile's Return: A literary Odyssey of the 1920s, 1951

Ernest Hemingway, A Moveable Feast, 1964

The Sun Also Rises, 1926

F. Scott Fitzgerald, The Beautiful and Damned, 1922

The Great Gatsby, 1925

Paula McLain, The Paris Wife, 2011

Mary Doria Russell, Dreamers of the Day, 2008

D. H. Lawrence, Women in Love, 1920

Edith Wharton, The Age of Innocence, 1920

Sinclair Lewis, Main Street, 1920

James Joyce, Ulysses, 1922

E. M. Forster, A Passage to India, 1924

George Orwell, Burmese Days, 1934

Theodore Dreiser, An American Tragedy, 1925

Virginia Woolf, Mrs. Dalloway, 1925

Thomas Wolfe, Look Homeward Angel, 1929

William Faulkner, The Sound and the Fury, 1929

A. A. Milne, Winnie-the-Pooh, 1926

Kahlil Gibran, The Prophet, 1923

A. Hitler, Mein Kampf, 1925

Eugene O'Neill—wrote three major plays during this decade: Desire Under the Elms, Anna Christie, and Strange Interlude

Gertrude Stein, <u>Matisse, Picasso, and Gertrude Stein,</u> 1912; <u>The Autobi-ography of Alice B. Toklas,</u> 1933; <u>Three Lives,</u> 1909

Edna St. Vincent Millay, <u>The Collected Poetry,</u> 1923

Virginia Woolf, <u>To the Lighthouse, Orlando, A Room of One's Own</u>—also written and published during this decade.

Sinclair Lewis, <u>Babbitt, Arrowsmith, Elmer Gantry</u>—also written and published during this decade.

HEMINGWAY'S KEY WEST AND CUBA
And His *The Old Man and the Sea*

For many artists, their personal lives are as engaging, provocative, and interesting as their art. Some clear examples are Leonardo da Vinci, Picasso, Maya Angelo, Georgia O'Keeffe, Eugene O'Neill, and Pat Conroy. In marked contrast, there are also perhaps equally as many artists in which their personal lives, while they shed light on their work, are not all that compelling. For example, T. S. Eliot, Wallace Stevens, Jane Austen, and Emily Dickinson led fairly normal, staid, reserved lives. Ernest Hemingway's life was anything but normal. There are many biographies, fictionalized biographic novels, movies, and other accounts that detail his tempestuous life. This essay will highlight some of the basic features of his life as a context for looking more closely at his time in Florida's Key West and Cuba. I conclude with an exploration of his magnificent novel, **The Old Man and the Sea**. On some level, all art is autobiographical. The artist wants us to view through the lens she or he is presenting, be it music, sculpture, poetry, painting, novel, or whatever. However, that lens is shaped and influenced, defined and determined by the life of that artist, no matter how removed the art is from directly reflecting that artist's life. Georgia O'Keeffe's flower or skull paintings tell us something profound and significant about her. The **Mona Lisa** tells us something about who Leonardo da Vinci was.

Hemingway's writings are dramatically shaped by his personal life—his stormy marriages to four wives, his tormented family's mental illnesses, his struggle with self-identity, his massive insecurities, and his passion to be famous. He had a very large and demanding ego. Thus, it is useful to understand Hemingway's works in the larger context of his life.

He was born Ernest Miller Hemingway on July 21, 1899 in Oak Park, Illinois to Dr. Clarence Hemingway, a physician, and Grace Hall Hemingway, a musician. Both parents were well educated and well respected in Oak Park, a rather conservative, Midwestern community about which Frank Lloyd Wright is to have said: "So many churches for so many good people to go." Upper middle class, the family also summer vacationed at a cottage it owned on Walloon Lake, near Petoskey, Michigan in northern Michigan—not far from where I live. His years there instilled a passion for hunting, fishing, and a love for the woods, lakes, and streams. The area shaped his Nick Adams short stories, which take place in northern Michigan. One of his best known is "The Big Two-Hearted River," published in 1925, which gave him credibility as a serious writer.

Ernest attended high school in Oak Park, where he participated in a number of sports, such as boxing, track, and football. He excelled in English and studied journalism. Like Mark Twain, Stephen Crane, Theodore Dreiser, and Sinclair Lewis, all noted American novelists that no doubt influenced Hemingway, he was a journalist before becoming a novelist. After high school, he was a reporter for the **Kansas City Star**. It was as a journalist that he honed his unique writing style: short, compact sentences; concise paragraphs; vigorous, active verbs; and a keep-it-simple approach that strives to be direct and to the point. These became known as his "iceberg theory" of writing fiction, which influenced many other writers.

In 1918, Ernest signed on to become an ambulance driver in Italy during WWI. On his way to Italy, he witnessed the bombing of Paris by the Germans. During this time, he met the well-known novelist John Dos Passos, with whom he became close friends. However, that friendship turned rocky and strained when Hemingway later attacked him. Over the course of his life, Hemingway had a pattern of attacking people who went out of their way to befriend, assist, and support him, such as Gertrude Stein, F. Scott Fitzgerald, and others. This pattern also clearly appears in his marriages. His personality seemed often to get in the way of sustained and healthy relationships.

His experiences in Italy during the war are effectively and vividly described in his novel, **A Farewell to Arms**, published in 1929. He is obviously impacted by the Red Cross workers picking up fragments of bodies. Seriously wounded by mortar fire on the front lines, Hemingway, only eighteen at the time, is sent to Milan to be treated in a Red Cross hospital. He was there for six months. He writes: "When you go to war as a boy you have the illusion of immortality. Other people get killed; not you…. Then when you are badly wounded the first time, you lose that illusion and you know it can happen to you." While in the hospital in Milan, he fell in love with a nurse seven years his senior. He wanted to marry her, and actual plans were initially made. However, she writes to him after he returns to the US that she had become engaged to an Italian officer. Hemingway was deeply rejected and hurt by this. One biographer argues that this rejection had such a lasting effect on him that he made sure he abandoned his wives before they abandoned him. This sheds some light on how he treats women in his novels and his life.

After his war experience and his broken heart, he returned home to Illinois in 1919 to recuperate. No job, no money, and uncomfortable living at home, he took a fishing and camping trip that September with some high-school friends to Michigan's Upper Peninsula. This trip became the inspiration for his Nick Adams short stories. He then moved to Toronto where he worked as a journalist for a weekly newspaper. Several months later he moved to Chicago, where he went to work as an editor for a monthly journal. Here he met the novelist Sherwood Anderson. While in Chicago, he also met Hadley Richardson from St. Louis, who came to Chicago to visit the sister of one of Hemingway's roommates. He immediately fell in love with Hadley. She was a stunning redhead, eight years older than he, and after a few months of passionate letter writing, they decided to marry and head for Europe. They were married in September of 1921; Hemingway was barely twenty-two. He was hired as a foreign correspondent for the **Toronto Star**. In the early years of their marriage, Ernest appeared very happy, for he had a beautiful woman at his side, had suitable income, and was living the bohemian life in Paris and traveling throughout Europe.

These were heady times for expatiates living in Paris at the time. Hemingway entered the inner circle of Gertrude Stein, the "Grande Dame" of literature in those days, and hobnobbed with Ezra Pound, James Joyce, Picasso, Joan Miro, and others. Gertrude Stein named the group "The Lost Generation," and they lived their lives attempting to live up to that reputation. She also mentored Ernest and helped him with early publications. She was very influential in his early success as a writer, though he later treated her with contempt in his memoir about those days in Paris, **A Moveable Feast**. While in Paris, he filed eighty-eight stories for the Toronto newspaper, covered the Greco-Turkish War, traveled to Spain, Italy, and elsewhere in Europe.

Back in Paris in 1924 after extensive travels, he and Hadley had their first son. He also had some of his short stories published, with the help of Stein and others. He then met and entered into a stormy relationship with F. Scott Fitzgerald and his wife Zelda. F. Scott had just published **The Great Gatsby**, which Hemingway admired. He decided that he, too, could write a novel, so he began to work on what was to become **The Sun Also Rises**, which was published by Scribner's in 1926 to immediate success. He signed a contract with Scribner. The novel describes the post-WWI expatriate Lost Generation in Europe and is considered by some of his critics as his best work.

During these days, while traveling, writing, and covering stories in Austria and elsewhere, he met Pauline Pfeiffer, with whom he began an affair. Once the affair became public, his marriage to Hadley quickly deteriorated. She asked for a separation and then a divorce, which happened in January of 1927. Hemingway and Pfeiffer married in May of that year. From a very wealthy, Catholic family, she moved to Paris to work for **Vogue** magazine. Hemingway converted to Catholicism, though never as a practicing member. Several successful short stories were published while living mainly in Paris. Pauline was pregnant and insisted they move back to the US. John Dos Passos recommended Key West, Florida, which is where they settled in 1928.

With plans to settle in Key West, they stopped in Kansas City, where Hemingway's second son, Patrick, was born on June 28, 1928. The very difficult delivery Pauline suffered becomes a part of his second novel, **A Farewell to Arms**, published to widespread critical acclaim. From Kansas City, the family traveled to Wyoming, Massachusetts, and New York, and were about to move permanently to Key West. While waiting to board a train in New York City, he received a cable telling him that his father had killed himself. Hemingway was devastated, even more so because he had recently written a letter to his father telling him not to worry about his own personal finances. The letter arrived after his father was already dead. Added to the trauma, Hemingway realized how Hadley, his first wife, must have felt when her father committed suicide in 1903. Hemingway wrote: "I'll probably go the same way," a sad but telling foreshadowing of his own end.

Ernest, Pauline, and son Patrick are now living in Key West. With the publication of the very well-received **The Sun Also Rises**, followed three years later by **A Farewell to Arms**, Hemingway enjoys financial and popular success as an established, major American writer. However, unable to settle down, Ernest leaves his family in Key West and travels to Spain to research his next book, **Death in the Afternoon**, his treatise on bullfighting, in which he maintains that "bullfighting was of great tragic interest, being literally of life and death." Hemingway was clearly attracted to the dangerous edges of life.

During the early 1930s, he is spending winters in Key West and summers and falls in Wyoming, where he hunted deer, elk, and bear. Dos Passos came to visit him in Wyoming to hunt. In November of 1930, while taking Dos Passos to the train station in Billings, Montana, Ernest broke his arm in a car accident. It took over a year to heal, during which time he suffered intense pain. In fact, the compound-fracture in his writing hand caused him difficulty the rest of his life. A year later, in 1931, his third son, Gregory, is born in Kansas City.

In 1933 Hemingway and Pauline went on an African safari for a ten-week hunting expedition. From this trip, he wrote and published the **Green Hills of Africa** as well as several short stories, including the well-known "The Snows of Kilimanjaro." While in Africa, he contracted amoebic dysentery, which caused him to be evacuated to Nairobi for treatment. He returned to Key West in 1934. That same year he purchased his famous boat, the **Pilar**, which he used for fishing and touring around the Caribbean.

When the Spanish Civil War broke out, Ernest signed a contract in 1937 to go to Spain to cover the story for the North American Newspaper Alliance. He was also hired to write a script for a film about the war, replacing Dos Passos as the writer and causing a rift in their long friendship. While in Spain, he met George Orwell, who was there fighting on the side of the rebels to overthrow Franco. It was also there that he hooked up with Martha Gellhorn, whom he had briefly met earlier in Key West and who was also in Spain to cover the war. Traveling back and forth between Key West and Spain in 1937 and 1938, Ernest was one of the last journalists to leave Spain at the end of the conflict when it was clear Franco was going to win. Supporters of the rebels where now seen as war criminals, and reporters sympathetic to their cause also faced arrest. Hemingway left Spain. Martha remained firmly imprinted in his heart and mind.

In 1939, Hemingway took his boat to Cuba. Martha joined him there, and he and Pauline began a long, drawn-out, bitter separation. With his second divorce final, he and Martha married on November 20, 1940 in Cheyenne, Wyoming. Under the strong influence of Martha Gellhorn, he began writing one of his most famous novels, **For Whom the Bell Tolls** (the title taken from a line in a seventeenth century poem by John Donne). He wrote it while in Cuba, Wyoming, and Idaho, where he had a summer residence close to the newly built and famous resort, Sun Valley. Published in October of 1940, less than four months after he began writing it, the novel became a Book-Of-The-Month-Club selection, sold a half a million copies within months, and nominated him for a Pulitzer Prize.

In January of 1941, celebrating his fame and financial success, he travels with Martha to China, who is on assignment for **Collier's** magazine. They returned to Cuba just before the US entered WWII. From May 1944 to March of 1945, Ernest was in London and regions of Europe as a war correspondent. While in London, he suffered a car accident that landed him in the hospital. This is one of several accidents Ernest had throughout his life. He appears to have been very accident-prone. In London, he fell in love with another correspondent, Mary Welsh. Martha and Ernest had a very contentious, often embittered relationship, where two strong, independent egos clashed. They divorced in March of 1945. He had already asked Mary Welsh to marry him after only meeting her on three occasions.

Present at the Normandy Landing, with a bandaged head from his car accident, he reported that he could see "the first, second, third, fourth, and fifth waves of landing troops lay where they had been fallen, looking like so many heavily laden bundles on the flat pebbly stretch between the sea and first cover." In July of 1945, he attached himself to a small band of militia in France as part of the Resistance to German occupation. He was there as a reporter but insisted on joining the fight. On August 25, 1944, he was present at the liberation of Paris. By this time, Mary Welsh had joined him in Paris. He then went to cover the Battle of the Bulge in Luxembourg, where he became very ill with a fever. He was hospitalized with pneumonia. He was awarded a Bronze Star for his bravery during WWII.

He married Mary Welsh, his fourth wife, in 1946, and the two lived mainly in Cuba and Idaho, though they traveled extensively. Hemingway confessed that he was "out of business as a writer" from 1942–1945 during his residence in Cuba. Shortly after they married, she suffered from an ectopic pregnancy. In fact, there were a whole series of accidents haunting the Hemingway family. He had another car accident in 1945, smashed his knee, suffered another head injury; Mary broke her right angle and then her left in two different skiing accidents; a 1947 car accident left son Patrick with a serious injury, and Ernest was battling a number of other illnesses.

He sank into a deep depression, intensified by seeing his literary friends beginning to grow old and die. Yeats and Ford Madox Ford died in 1939; F. Scott Fitzgerald in 1940; Sherwood Anderson and James Joyce in 1941; Gertrude Stein in 1946; and in 1947 his longtime friend and editor for Scribner's, Maxwell Perkins, died. Ernest was suffering during these years with severe headaches, high blood pressure, weight problems; struggling with diabetes; and years of heavy drinking added to his health problems and his depression. He felt abandoned, alone, unable to concentrate on writing, and he feared he had lost his creative capacities.

In 1948, he and Mary traveled to Europe, staying for several months in Venice. While there, he fell madly in love with a nineteen-year-old woman, who flirted and teased him but made him realize the relationship could never work. She made him feel very old. His marriage to Mary was on very shaky ground. To get away from it all, Ernest takes his second trip to Africa with Mary, where they stayed for a couple of years. While in Africa, he survived two plane crashes, one of which almost took his life. Mary broke her ribs in one of these. News of the accidents led some reporters to claim that he had been killed in a plane crash. There even appeared some obituaries about him. Despite his injuries and acute pain, he, Mary, and son Patrick go on a fishing expedition. The trip was a disaster due to the intense pain and physical limitations of Ernest. During this expedition, a brushfire broke out, resulting in severe burns and other injuries to Ernest. While recuperating back in Venice months later, Mary reported to friends that Ernest's injuries included: two cracked discs, a kidney and liver rupture, a dislocated shoulder, and a broken skull. To combat his pain, he took to drinking more heavily than usual and probably was also taking pain medications.

In October 1954, he was awarded the Nobel Prize in Literature. Due to his physical condition, he was not able to travel to Stockholm to receive the prize. In his acceptance speech, he defines a writer's life as follows: "Writing, at its best, is a lonely life. Organizations for writers palliate the writer's loneliness but I doubt if they improve his writing. He grows in public stature as he sheds his loneliness and often his work deteriorates. For he does his work alone and if he is a good enough writer he must face eternity, or the lack of it, each day."

Hemingway was clearly haunted by acute loneliness, a sustained sense of failure, and now a growing awareness of his own mortality. From the end of 1955 to early 1956, he was virtually bedridden. He was told by doctors to stop drinking, advice he disregarded. In October of 1956, he returns to Europe but was still suffering from multiple illnesses. In November of that year, he is staying again in Paris. He remembered that he had stored trunks of manuscripts and other items at the Ritz Hotel in Paris from way back in 1928. He retrieved the trunks and found that they were full of notebooks and writings from his earlier Paris years. Eagerly he returns to Cuba in 1957 and begins writing his famous memoir, **A Moveable Feast**, published in 1959. This was also a period of intense writing in which he tried to prove to himself and the world that he still had creative juices.

Despite these efforts to write and amidst continued physical deterioration, pain, and heavy drinking, he sunk deeper into depression. He returned to Spain in mid-1959 to research a series of bullfighting articles for **Life** magazine, which resulted in a full-length book that was not well received. He was also suffering from failing eyesight. In the summer of 1960, after leaving Cuba for good, he set up a small apartment in New York City, with the hopes of writing again. He returned briefly to Spain, where he became very ill. He returned to Mary in New York, and she took him to their summer place in Idaho, where Dr. George Saviers, a well-known Sun Valley physician, met them at the train.

Given his depression, acute paranoia set in. Ernest worried about never getting the manuscripts he left in Cuba, he worried about money, taxes, his health, reputation, creativity, and on and on and on. He believed the FBI was going to steal his manuscripts from Cuba and that the FBI was watching him in Ketchum, Idaho. There was some credibility for this, because the FBI had opened a file on him during WWII. Facing her own stresses, Mary, following the advice of Dr. Saviers, takes Ernest to the Mayo Clinic in December of 1960. While there, he was treated with electro-shock therapy as many as fifteen times, leaving him in physical ruins. There is some speculation that the medications and treatment accelerated and intensified his depression and sense of paranoia.

In April of 1961, three months after returning to Idaho from the Mayo Clinic, Mary finds Ernest holding a shotgun in the kitchen one morning. In a panic, she calls Dr. Saviers, who heavily sedates him, admits him to the Sun Valley Hospital and then back to the Mayo Clinic for more electroshock treatments. Hemingway is by now feeling that his life is totally out of his own control, for he is suffering from acute pain and depression and he knows that his physical conditions will only get worse. He returns to Ketchum, Idaho on June 30, 1961. On the morning of July 2 of that year, he deliberately put a shotgun to his head and pulled the trigger. Mary heard the shot, called a doctor, who came to the home and acknowledged that he died of a self-inflicted wound to the head. Five years later Mary admitted that her husband killed himself.

Family and friends flooded to Ketchum for the funeral, which was conducted by a local priest, who maintained Ernest's death to be accidental. He was buried in the Ketchum cemetery. During these sad, painful end-of-life years, Ernest suffered from a mental disorder that his father had been diagnosed with. Medical records reveal that Ernest was diagnosed with the same genetic disorder in early 1961. In addition to the suicide of his father, his sister Ursula and his brother Leicester also killed themselves. In 1966 a memorial to Ernest Hemingway was placed outside of Sun Valley, above Trail Creek, with the following words Ernest had written much earlier for a friend:

> Best of all he loved the fall
> The leaves yellow on cottonwoods
> Leaves floating on trout steams
> and above the hills
> the high blue windless skies.
> ....*Now he will be a part of them forever.*

HEMINGWAY IN KEY WEST, FLORIDA

With his second wife Pauline, who is pregnant with Patrick, the Hemingway family left Paris and settled in Key West via a trip to Havana on April 7, 1928. They first settled into an apartment. Ernest was preoccupied with writing **A Farewell to Arms**. In addition to writing, Ernest spent his time fishing in the waters off Key West. He and Pauline became friends with several locals, including Joe Russell, owner of the famous Sloppy Joe's Saloon. Other friends included a liquor smuggler, an attorney, and several well-known fishing buddies. The circle of friends fished off the coast of Cuba, Bimini, the Keys, and elsewhere and became known as the Key West "Mob," calling Ernest "Papa." They returned to Key West every winter from 1928 to 1939. Hemingway was twenty-nine when he first settled there.

In April of 1931, they purchased a large, Spanish-styled house at 907 Whitehead Street, with the help of Pauline's uncle, for $12,500. This became his main residence in Key West until he leaves Pauline. Ernest left Pauline and moved to Cuba with his new wife Martha Gellhorn. Pauline and her sons remained in the Key West house until her death in 1951. After Hemingway's death in July of 1961, his estate sold the property. It became and still is a major attraction in Key West, known as The Hemingway House.

He often left Key West for hunting trips to Africa, bullfights in Spain, and other travels. The house had the first swimming pool in Key West, which cost $20,000. The story goes that Ernest told the contractor—"Here, take my last penny," which he embedded in the wet concrete at the north end of the pool. The story is also told that while in Paris, he and Pauline were guests of a local member of the artist set hanging out in Paris. The host had cats that would jump up on the dining table while people were eating and nibble off the plates. Hemingway was aghast at this. Interestingly, he and Pauline proceeded to fill their new home with cats, and many of their offspring are supposedly still there today. He also had cats at his Cuban estate.

Several of his books were written during his Key West days, and local characters can be found in these works. They include: **Green Hills of Africa, Death in the Afternoon, To Have and Have Not**, as well as a number of short stories. He was a local celebrity, not only for his writing, but also for his prowess as a fisherman and drinker. In 1934, he purchased his own fishing boat, which he named **Pilar**. John Dos Passos, who suggested living in Key West, frequently visited the Hemingways during these days. After marrying Martha Gellhorn in 1940, he never lived there again, though he did visit occasionally. By the way, he first met Martha at Sloppy Joe's bar in December of 1936, and they became lovers and traveling companions during the Spanish Civil War in 1937. Interestingly, his wife Pauline at the time supported Franco's Fascist government, because she was Catholic. Ernest and Martha supported the communist loyalists who were battling for a democratic government. The Key West lifestyle, climate, people, and the fishing all had strong attractions for Ernest, as did the rugged mountains of Wyoming and Idaho. He often balanced his time between Key West and then Cuba and his summer residence outside of Sun Valley, Idaho.

HEMINGWAY IN CUBA

If the laid-back, casual lifestyle, the carousing and drinking, the fishing, the climate, and the tight circle of "good-old-boys" suited Hemingway during his days in Key West, he was even more attracted to Cuba for all the same reasons. Of course, he also saw Cuba as an escape from the political scene in the US during the early 1940s as well as escape from Pauline, his second wife. While in Key West, he was not very attentive to her or the children. He lived part time in Cuba from 1939–1960. He married his third wife, Martha, in 1940, and she was with him frequently in Cuba and on his many travel adventures. As an internationally famous writer and personality, Cuba welcomed Ernest with open arms.

He purchased a home there, named "Finca Vigia," which means "Lookout Farm" and which was located in a quiet, remote hamlet of San Francisco de Paula. This fifteen-acre property, unusually large by Cuban standards, is about fifteen miles from Havana. Pauline and the children left Ernest in the summer of 1940. She refused to compete with Martha. Like The Hemingway House in Key West, Finca Vigia is also a huge tourist attraction, owned by the Cuban government. It was built in 1886 by a well-known architect. Hemingway bought it in 1940 at the urging of his wife Pauline, who did not want to stay in a hotel in Havana.

His marriage to Martha only lasted from November of 1940 until 1945, when he married his fourth and final wife, Mary Welsh. Mary ran the Cuban household for fifteen years as a winter resident. Ernest wrote most of **For Whom the Bell Tolls** and **The Old Man and the Sea** while in Cuba. After his death, the Cuban government informed Mary that it had confiscated all of the property and that it was now a national treasure, including letters, manuscripts, and other personal holdings. With the help of her friend Jackie Kennedy, Mary was able to retrieve the manuscripts, which are now housed in the Kennedy Library in Boston. Most of the personal effects, such as clothing, photographs, and other private items, remained in the house. As one writer noted on a pilgrimage to the Cuban shrine in 2017, our group was clearly informed by our guide that while we are visiting Hemingway's home, "we are in a Communist Country where journalists are not welcomed." For its time, the house was very elegant and comfortable but small. The rooms have high ceilings and are open and airy. Much of the furniture, mostly of dark wood, was commissioned by Mary.

While living in both Key West and Cuba, Ernest fashioned himself as an affable and popular celebrity. With engaging hunting and fishing stories, he was clearly living a life of heavy drinking and partying. A government brochure boasts that Charlie Chaplin, Ava Gardner, and other famous celebrities visited him in Cuba. His leather boots, worn jackets, mounted animal heads of antelope, a huge water buffalo, other trophies of his many hunts, and other personal effects remain in place. Some see signs of valor, exciting expeditions, and daring exploits, others may view the mounted heads as crimes against nature. At the estate in Cuba there are reminders of a great writer with a high degree of pathos and sadness—a life lived to its fullest but one also filled with pain, suffering, and ultimately a self-inflicted death. John Updike wrote this about Hemingway: "Celebrity is a mask that eats into the face"—an all-too-accurate statement. By the time he moved to Cuba, he was trapped by his own reputation.

A life of danger, living on the edge, violence, constant threats of death, many accidents and illnesses, along with his inherited mental disease, Ernest Hemingway was able to write about all of these with intense and magnetic clarity. He sought all these out as material for his writings. They fed his hungry soul and captivated his creative force. However, by the time he settled winters in both Key West and Cuba, his life was no longer capable of seeking out the thrills and challenges that gave energy to his writing. The lovely, comfortable retreat in Cuba, complete with a swimming pool, tennis court, guest house, a staff of servants, was a place for entertainment. And indeed, the rich and famous frequently came to be entertained. The irony of all this is that Ernest felt acutely his own loss of creative prowess during these times. He felt time was running out. The Big Hunts and Quests for the Big Fish were over.

Although he and Martha and then Mary lived winters in Cuba on and off for over twenty years, also, like in Key West, filled with their beloved cats and trophies, his island lifestyle was taking a heavy toll. During the start of WWII, he would troll the Caribbean from his boat the **Pilar** looking for German subs and U-Boats. In 1944 he traveled back to Europe to cover WWII. It was on this trip, with a stopover in London, that he met Mary Welsh, who would become his fourth and final wife. They traveled throughout Europe together during the war. Divorcing Martha in 1945, he returns to Cuba in 1946 and then marries Mary. Cuba's deterioration following the 1959 revolution caused the Hemingways to leave it in 1960. One year later he committed suicide.

Most of his last great book, **The Old Man and the Sea**, was written while living in Cuba. It was originally published in 1952 in its entirety in **Life** magazine. Sales exceeded all expectations. In 1953 he was honored with a Pulitzer Prize. And in 1954 he was awarded the Nobel Prize for literature. I personally consider **The Old Man and the Sea** to be one of his greatest novel, if not his greatest. It deserves our attention.

THE OLD MAN AND THE SEA

This concise, simple, direct, compact, short novel appears, on the surface, to be merely a fishing adventure story. In marked contrast with his contemporary writers, such as James Joyce, William Faulkner, F. Scott Fitzgerald, and many others, Hemingway perfects his "iceberg" theory of writing in this novel—free of flowery adjectives, spartan in its delivery, short, staccato sentences, and a straightforward narrative. His last major novel to be published while still alive, it tells the story of an old Cuban fisherman, Santiago, who goes far out in the Gulf Stream off the coast of Cuba and hooks a giant marlin. Hemingway was proud of the marlins he caught fishing, some of whom he had mounted. Santiago, an experienced but aging fisherman, has gone eighty-four days without catching a fish, suffering from "Salao," the worst form of unluckiness.

Manolin, the young boy who usually fishes with Santiago, is forbidden by his parents to go fishing with Santiago because of his bad luck. The boy visits Santiago's shack each night, helping him with his gear, preparing food, and talking about American baseball, especially Joe DiMaggio. Santiago tells the boy that the next day he will venture way out in the Gulf Stream and end his bad luck. On his eighty-fifth day, Santiago takes his small fishing skiff way out to sea, sets his baited lines, and has a strike by what he knows is a huge fish. Unable to haul in the giant marlin, he is pulled for two days and two nights by the fish, with Santiago desperately hanging on to the line. Facing the pain of exhaustion, the old man reflects on his appreciation and compassion for this magnificent creature, reminiscent of Ishmael's reference for the great white whale in **Moby Dick**. Referring to him as his spiritual brother, Santiago is determined that no one will capture this fish, admiring its dignity and determination to survive.

On the third day, the fish begins circling the skiff. Almost delirious, Santiago manages finally to pull the marling into the boat and stabs him with his harpoon. Strapping the marlin to the side of his boat, he heads for home thinking about all the money the fish will bring, plus his own fame and all the people of his village it will feed. However, drawn by the blood of the fish, sharks attack the marlin. Santiago kills one shark with his harpoon but loses it in the process. He fashions another harpoon by strapping his knife to an oar. He strikes five other sharks and drives others away. But the sharks keep coming and by nightfall they have devoured most of the marlin, leaving a skeleton of its backbone, tail and head. Defeated, out of energy, suffering from exhaustion, Santiago tells the marlin that the sharks have killed his dreams. He reaches shore and carries the heavy mast of the boat on his shoulders to his shack, leaving the marlin's remaining skeleton tied to his boat. He falls into a deep sleep in his shack.

A group of fishermen gather around the old man's boat the next day and notice the skeleton still lashed to the boat. It measures eighteen feet from head to tail. One of the fishermen takes the head of the fish, another tells Manolin the boy to go find Santiago and tell him how sorry they are. Tourists from a nearby café gather around the fish thinking it is a giant shark. Manolin brings Santiago newspapers and coffee. When the old man wakes up, Manolin promises him that he will fish with him again. Falling back asleep, Santiago dreams of his youth and of lions on the beach of Africa.

Packed with allegorical and religious symbolism, the novel dramatically illustrates the human drive for survival. One important passage that gives evidence of this from the book reads: "Ay, he said aloud. There is no translation for this word and perhaps it is just a noise such as a man might make, involuntarily, feeling the nail go through his hand and into the wood." Some critics correctly see this as a direct reference to Christ's crucifixion. Further, Manolin has Christ-like overtones, and Santiago's name has Christian implications. Like Christ laboring under the cross, Santiago carries the heavy mast from his boat back to his hut. He then collapses on his bed exhausted and lays spread eagle with his arms stretched out cross-like. These Christian references invite the reader to consider an almost mystical transcendence from defeat to triumph, loss to gain, death to renewed life.

The major theme of the novel is the heroism of Santiago, his determination against all odds, his ability to endure hunger, pain, and exhaustion, and his capacity to survive acute loneliness. He is a classic example of Hemingway's belief in "grace under pressure." He does not blame the sharks for attacking the marlin. He does admit his own mistake in venturing out too far from shore. But we see a man driven to overcome his defeat—eighty-four days with no fish, mocked by the villagers and fellow fishermen, and the parents of Manolin forbidding him to go fishing with him. Far out to sea, way beyond where he should have gone, totally drained and fighting pain and abandonment, he wards off defeat by recalling his youth and the dreams he had as a boy of lions on the beach in Africa. And he prays for help, for strength.

In the end, protecting the marlin from the sharks is not his ultimate goal. It is his own survival—his heroic determination to make it back. He states at the end of the novel: "a man can be destroyed but not defeated." Hemingway presents him as a man driven to survive. He represents a person that goes beyond victory over these incredible odds, a person who struggles and wins. In the process, Santiago gains deep insight into himself and his relationship with the sea, the village, and other people. The sea is often described in terms of a woman who both gives and takes. Santiago comes to love the natural world in which he lives—the sea, the marlin, and even the sharks. In fact, the marlin, like Moby Dick, takes on spiritual dimensions—a kind of sacred entity even seen as his brother. Heading for home, he has a sense of guilt for killing the marlin, a sense of loneliness. He realizes he has killed something he has come to love. He ends up with a kind of emptiness. Yet he survives to fish again, significantly with his young assistant, Manolin. Both remain inspired by the great Joe DiMaggio, and both are bonded by renewed life.

Tightly crafted with direct, simple, short sentences, and vivid imagery, Hemingway writes a classic story for all times and all ages. It is a powerful illustration of our human dignity, strength, and determination, regardless of odds that seem insurmountable. Although often considered by many to be essentially a man's writer and a man's man, Hemingway touches themes that resonate with our fundamental humanity. These are themes of love, war, loss, survival, strength against overwhelming odds, and the ever-present awareness of nature as our eternal and sacred context. He clearly left a very large footprint on the landscape of American literature and, indeed, all of Western literature. He has a legendary presence. Macho, to be sure, Hemingway clearly was attracted to wars, big-game hunting, deep-sea fishing, bullfighting, boxing, drinking, and carousing with the boys. His writings reflect this macho attraction. Nevertheless, he also possessed a forceful, appealing, and engaging personality. He could be charming, magnetic, and entertaining. He could also be maddening, insulting, and even vindictive. While his life continues to be fascinating, it is his creative achievements as a writer that will live on as important contributions to Western literature, giving that literature a distinctive and effective American voice.

HEMINGWAY TIMELINE: SOME IMPORTANT DATES

> **July 21, 1899,** born in Oak Park, Illinois.
> **1918:** joins the Red Cross, traveling to Paris and then to Milan, Italy during WWI; wounded by mortar shell; discharged in 1919; returns to US; received Italian Silver Medal for bravery.
> **1921–1927:** Marries Hadley Richardson; they move to Paris; meets Gertrude Stein in 1922 and other artists, including Ezra Pound and James Joyce; publishes short stories; meets F. Scott Fitzgerald in Paris

in 1925; publishes "Big Two-Hearted River;" publishes first novel, THE SUN ALSO RISES IN 1926; divorces Hadley Richardson in 1927 while still in Paris and marries Pauline Pfeiffer back in the US that same year.

> **1928–1939:** Lives winters in Key West, Florida; purchases the house with wife Pauline; father commits suicide in 1928; second son Patrick born in 1928; publishes A FAREWELL TO ARMS in 1929; travels extensively to Spain, Africa, and elsewhere in Europe; third son Gregory born in 1931. Spends summers often in Ketchum, Idaho. *DEATH IN THE AFTERNOON*, book about bullfighting in Spain, published in 1932; publishes memoir, *GREEN HILLS OF AFRICA*, 1935. Goes to Spain in 1937 as a reporter to cover Spanish Civil War.

> **1939–1960:** Lives winters in Cuba; publishes *FOR WHOM THE BELL TOLLS* in 1940; continues extensive travels to Europe, Africa, elsewhere.

> **1940:** Divorces Pauline Pfeiffer; marries Martha Gellhorn.

> **1944:** WWII correspondent for **Collier's Magazine**; present at the liberation of Paris.

> **1945:** Divorces Martha Gellhorn.

> **1946–1954:** Marries Mary Welsh in 1946; publishes THE OLD MAN AND THE SEA in 1952.
  Awarded the Pulitzer Prize for his fiction in 1953 and in 1954 awarded Nobel Prize for literature.

> **July 2, 1961:** Ends his life at his home in Ketchum, Idaho.

NOTABLE QUOTATIONS

> "There is nothing noble in being superior to your fellow man; true nobility is being superior to your former self."

> "The world breaks everyone, and afterward, some are strong at the broken places."

> "There is nothing to writing. All you do is sit down at a typewriter and bleed."

> "Courage is grace under pressure."

> "But man is not made for defeat. A man can be destroyed but not defeated."

HEMINGWAY'S TOP FOUR NOVELS

THE SUN ALSO RISES, 1926: Based on his life in Paris and Spain, the story is about a group of Americans and British men and women in the post-WWII era living self-indulged, hedonistic lives in Paris as expatriates. They travel from Paris to Pamplona, Spain to experience the famous annual festival of the running of the bulls and the bullfights. The main character is Jake Barnes, who also narrates the story. He and Lady Brett Ashley are in love. Due to Jake's war wound, which leaves him impotent, their relationship is tested. Sordid living, heavy drinking, betrayal, affairs, and tested relationships drive the novel. These are contrasted by Hemingway's passionate admiration for Spain, its culture, and the drama of bullfighting.

A FAREWELL TO ARMS, 1929: Also highly autobiographical, this is a story of Frederic Henry, who is an American lieutenant and the narrator of the novel. Like Hemingway, he is wounded by a mortar shell while serving as an ambulance driver in the Italian Army during WWI. He falls in love with Catherine Barkley, an English nurse. The novel describes the trials and challenges of their love in the context of the war. They eventually end up together, but she dies in childbirth at the end of the novel, leaving Frederic alone and despondent.

FOR WHOM THE BELL TOLLS, 1940: Again, highly autobiographical, this novel is set during the Spanish Civil War. It tells the story of Robert Jordan, who is an American experienced explosive expert in the International Brigade fighting against fascism. It's also a dramatic love story of Robert and Maria, who is also a rebel fighter. Honor, duty, camaraderie, love, innocence, courage, death, and sacrifice are all big thematic concepts played out in the story. Robert's job is to blow up strategically important bridges. It graphically describes the brutality of war in general and this war in particular. It ends with Jordan hoping for one last shot at the enemy before he dies.

THE OLD MAN AND THE SEA, 1952: The last major work written and published in his lifetime. {Covered in the essay.}

HIS MAJOR MEMOIRS

DEATH IN THE AFTERNOON, 1932: A passionate description of Spanish bullfighting—its ceremonies and traditions, its cultural importance to Spain, and as a metaphor for life.

GREEN HILLS OF AFRICA, 1935: Hemingway's safari with Pauline in Africa.

A MOVEABLE FEAST, 1964: Hemingway's account of the "Lost Generation" of expatriates in Paris during the 1920s.

A LITERARY GIANT
The Life and Works of John Steinbeck

How do we begin to wrap our minds around the works of John Steinbeck, a gigantic literary talent? His work ranges far and wide over a diverse landscape, with some of them as huge achievements displaying his creative genius, while others fall flat, like **The Winter of Our Discontent**. The sheer volume of his published works speaks to his capacity and capability. He published over forty books, including sixteen novels, eleven books of nonfiction, two collections of short stories, screenplays, journals, essays, and many, many letters. He also published a collection of articles from his career as a journalist. He is best known, of course, for his novels. Several of his works are set in the Salinas Valley, around Monterrey and the surrounding areas.

There are multiple versions of the famous "Red Pony" stories, which are woven together into a compelling account about the inevitability of death and a boy's coming of age in facing this inevitability. The emerging power of Steinbeck's voice shines with these stories. **Of Mice and Men**, published in 1937, also became a successful play on Broadway and a movie. Steinbeck's popular characters, George Milton and Lennie Small, as the odd couple, were exceedingly popular. Steinbeck calls this novella "a little study in humility." It is an enticing story about these two displaced migrant ranch workers in California during the Great Depression. The presence of acute loneliness and isolation runs through this work as the main characters move from place to place searching for work. The title is taken from a Robert Burns poem, "To a Mouse," which reads: "The best laid schemes o' mice an' men often go awry."

Of Mice and Men and **In Dubious Battle** both set the stage for his masterpiece, **The Grapes of Wrath**. **In Dubious Battle** is one of the best novels ever written about labor organizing, strikes, abuses of power, and farm workers in the 1930s. The tradition of this novel is continued by the contemporary, historical novel by Mary Doria Russell, entitled **Women of the Copper Country** (2019). **The Moon is Down**, published in 1942, was also adapted for the theater and won a major award in Norway for the production. The story is a moving, powerful, and painful account of the military occupation of a small town in northern Europe, clearly referencing the Nazi occupation of Norway. It was published secretly in Germany and translated into several languages during the war, including Norwegian, Danish, Dutch, and Italian. It was also very popular in Russia. Set in a picturesque village in winter, the peaceful winter scene turns quickly to confusion, anger, and violence as the villagers are forced to obey the invader's commands. Ironically, Steinbeck depicts the disillusionment of the occupying soldiers, who want the war to end so they can go home and who do not understand why they are in this small village. The title comes from Shakespeare's **Macbeth**, in which Fleance says to Banquo: "The moon is down; I have not heard the clock."

A closer look at one of the greatest American novels, **The Grapes of Wrath**, reveals the incredible talent of this American icon. This well-known story is set during the Great Depression of the 1930s. The Joad family is struggling as tenant farmers in Oklahoma. Trapped by the hopelessness of their economic plight, their situation becomes even more dire when a dust storm hits the area, ruining any chance of making it as farmers. Along with many other "Okies," the Joads pack their rickety Hudson and head for California, seeking dignity, work, and opportunity. They believe in the promise of the American Dream. Tom Joad had just been paroled from prison and goes home only to find it abandoned. He finds his family at Uncle John's place, where they are packing the car and getting ready to leave. Although going with the family violates his parole, Tom, along with the ex-preacher Jim Casy, joins the family's journey on Route 66 for California. The road is crowded with other migrants, setting up makeshift camps, exchanging stories, and helping one another as best they can—all hoping to find a better life.

Grandpa Joad dies along the way. Grandma also dies just before reaching California. Noah, the eldest Joad son, and Connie Rivers, the husband of Rose of Sharon, the daughter who is pregnant, both leave the family. Ma Joad is determined to hold the remaining family together as they push on to California. After many setbacks and a very difficult journey, the Joads finally reach California, only to discover that the farm labor market is overflooded, wages are low, and the big farmers are brutally exploiting the workers. The big corporate farms seek to push out the smaller farmers by lowering the prices. Weedpatch Camp, one of the many New Deal efforts to assist the displaced workers, is overcrowded way beyond capacity. It does its best to protect and assist the migrants. This is all effectively captured in the novel.

Jim Casy, the ex-preacher and Tom's friend, becomes a farmworker organizer and tries to establish a labor union. The remaining Joads are working in a peach orchard. To preserve their jobs, they oppose the strike Casy has organized. The strike turns violent. Tom Joad witnesses the brutal and fatal beating of Casy, and he kills the attacker. Forced to flee as a fugitive, the Joad family, with Tom, leave the peach orchard and go to work on a cotton farm. To avoid being arrested, Tom bids farewell to the family, promising to work for the oppressed.

Rose of Sharon's baby is stillborn. Ma Joad remains determined to keep the family together. She is the rock of hope and family survival. Heavy rains flood them out. Forced to take shelter is an abandoned barn, they discover a young boy and his father, both of whom are starving to death. Rose of Sharon nurses the man with her breast milk to save him from starvation. The novel ends with that touching scene. This famous passage from the book captures the anguish, pathos, and despair: "How can you frighten a man whose hunger is not only in his own cramped stomach but in the wretched bellies of his children? You can't scare him—he has known fear beyond every other."

At the suggestion of his first wife, Carol, Steinbeck settles on the title from a line in "The Battle Hymn of the Republic," which reads:

> Mine eyes have seen the glory of the coming of the Lord:
> He is trampling out the vintage where the grapes of wrath are stored;
> He hath loosed the fateful lightning of His terrible swift sword:
> His truth is marching on....

Clearly, Steinbeck's title is an important indicator of a major theme—the terrible oppression the migrants face. The suffering is relentless. Steinbeck stated about this novel: "I want to put a tag of shame on the greedy bastards who are responsible for the Great Depression and its effects." And he goes on to say: "I've done my damnedest to rip a reader's nerves to rags." This novel was enormously embraced by the working class due to Steinbeck's overt sympathy for them. In addition to the title, there are many Biblical or Christian images in the book. Tom Joad and Jim Casy are both Christ-like figures. Ma Joad, Rose of Sharon, and Uncle John have clear religious overtones. The entire migration West is symbolic of the Jews escape from Egypt. And there are other Biblical references in the novel.

The Grapes of Wrath is a big, bold, brash book that climaxes his labor trilogy novels, which include **To a God Unknown** and **In Dubious Battle**. It was an enormous success, earning Steinbeck a Pulitzer Prize and contributing later to his Nobel Prize. It was the best-selling novel of 1939, with over 430,000 copies sold, winning Steinbeck the National Book Award. The movie, which came out in 1940, a year after publication, was also a huge success and it still is. Like the novel, both are considered classic American works of art. It has entered our social and political consciousness, much like **Uncle Tom's Cabin**. Steinbeck invites the reader to see the displaced and exploited migrants from the inside, to empathize with their plight, to feel their pain and losses, to share their struggle for dignity and respect. If the American Dream is a reality for many of Steinbeck's readers of this novel, he is exposing the harsh reality that the Dream is limited and not available for many others. The journey West does not open doors for a better life, does not enable the recreation of the Garden of Eden, does not bring dignity and respect, decency and opportunity.

The plight of the Joads and all the other migrants is, for Steinbeck, the new American Tragedy. Common, hardworking, decent folks face conditions that render them powerless. The power of that message still resonates today, perhaps even more so in these troubling, divisive times. 50,000 copies of **The Grapes of Wrath** are still sold every year, a testament to its importance. Many American high school students still read it as part of their curriculum. More than 15 million copies have been sold since its publication over eighty years ago. The impact of this novel is still very large indeed. Harry Belafonte once reported that Steinbeck's novels turned his life around and gave him a lifelong love of literature. The playwright Arthur Miller wrote: "I can't think of another American writer, with the possible exception of Mark Twain, who so deeply penetrated the political life of the country." Like **Moby Dick**, Steinbeck's masterpiece deserves to be read and reread several times. It is a magical, magnificent, masterful story, written with white-hot passion and infused with the creative power of Steinbeck's poetic voice that pleads for justice and opportunity.

Given the fact that so many of Steinbeck's books deal with the down-and-outers, the oppressed and exploited, the working class, the migrants, all pitted against the rich and powerful, you might think Steinbeck grew up poor. Not so. He grew up in Salinas in a beautiful Victorian house with maids and servants. He traveled first class. His father was the treasurer of Monterey County and his mother was a school teacher for a time. He grew up Episcopal, though later confessed that he was agnostic. Nevertheless, Christian images are very evident in his writings. Growing up in a solidly upper middle-class environment, he worked summers on area ranches and farms, mingling easily with the migrant workers.

He attended Stanford University but did not graduate, lived for a time in New York City, but returned to California, where he meets Carol Henning. They married in January of 1930. He had recently published his first novel, **The Cup of Gold**. Still not able to make a living as a writer, his parents allowed John and Carol to stay in their cottage on the Monterey Peninsula, not exactly a shabby place to hang out. While working on his second novel, **Cannery Row**, he fished, crabbed, tended a vegetable garden, and, for a time, depended on welfare. This was the Depression.

In 1930 he met and became a lifelong friend of Ed Ricketts, who introduced Steinbeck to philosophy, biology, environmentalism, and the ecological interdependence of all living things. Ricketts operated a lab on the Monterey coast, published essays, and a book, and gathered extensive samples of small fish, animals, and other marine forms. Not only were they close friends, but Ricketts played an important role in getting Steinbeck over his frequent bouts of depression. They collaborated on some works together, and Ricketts was the model for the character "Doc" in **Cannery Row**. Ricketts died in 1948, a real loss to Steinbeck.

John Steinbeck was an angry man, which contributed to his periods of depression. Complicated and contradictory, he was outraged by injustices, poverty, and prejudice. His books make that clear. Like Hemingway, he also frequently suffered from illnesses and accidents. At age sixteen, he almost died from pneumonia. He also had kidney infections, had surgery due to a detached retina, shattered his kneecap, struggled with back pain, and numerous other ailments. In 1959 at the age of fifty-seven, he had a stroke; and in 1960, he had a heart attack.

With the fame that came from **The Grapes of Wrath**, at age forty-one, Steinbeck falls in love with a twenty-two-year-old nightclub singer, named Gwyn Conger, with whom he had two children. He divorced his first wife, Carol, and married Gwyn in 1943. She divorced him in 1948. Many years after the divorce, she gave a series of interviews about her life with John. These interviews remained unpublished until they were accidently discovered in a loft in Wales in 2017. Dicey material, the interviews were published as a book in 2018, titled **My Life with John Steinbeck**. This tell-all memoir describes a man capable of viciousness toward his children and his wife and his serious drinking problems that often led to cruelty. She shows us an unpleasant side, claiming he was sadistic. Although Steinbeck was long gone when this book came out, he was well aware of Gwyn's many efforts to discredit him in public and to expose the uglier side of him. He gets back at her by creating Cathy, the wicked, manipulative whore in **East of Eden**. Although this unsavory account of Steinbeck was published long after his death, there were other articles and accounts of his treatment of women during his lifetime. A year after the publication of the highly acclaimed **Grapes of Wrath**, he hit bottom and sought psychological treatment. He continued to suffer from what he called "what-the-hell-blues." These bouts of depression continued even after he met and married his third wife, Elaine Scott. One of the puzzling contradictions about Steinbeck was his political shift from progressive liberalism to strong support for the Vietnam War. He was certainly progressive about race relations. He insisted that his name be removed from a screenplay he wrote for Alfred Hitchcock because the movie distorted and stereotyped the black character Steinbeck had created. He often associated with and supported left-leaning authors, journalists, and political activists, especially voicing his strong support for labor unions. He even had some very loose association with members of the American Communist Party. In 1957, Steinbeck took a personal and professional risk by supporting Arthur Miller's refusal to name names in the House Un-American Activities Committee hearings under Joseph McCarthy. Steinbeck called the hearings one of the "strangest and most frightening times a government and people have ever faced." He also frequently complained that the FBI was targeting him for suspicious activities.

However, in 1967 he is sent to Vietnam as a war correspondent at age sixty-five, a year before his death, reporting for the **New York Post**. He actively endorses the war efforts, becomes a friend of President Lyndon Johnson, and is angered when his sons turn against the war after serving in Vietnam. In fact, Steinbeck helps Johnson with his acceptance speech. He wrote that the peace protesters gave him "a shiver of shame." And he attacked hippie demonstrators for their "dirty clothes and dirty minds."

His two sons, Thomas and John IV, struggled with their relationship with their father, who was sometimes very demanding and abusive toward them. Thomas died at age seventy-two and he tried to make it as a writer without much success. After his father died, he fought bitterly with the family over his father's estate. John IV became actively opposed to the Vietnam War, after his tour in the military in Vietnam. He, too, struggled as a writer. His anti-Vietnam position estranged him from his father, which was never resolved.

I confess that **East of Eden** is my favorite Steinbeck novel and one of my all-time most admired works. I rank it in the top ten of all American novels. Challenging to read with its sweeping span of people, spaces, plots, and sub-plots, it is ambitious, prophetic, loud, bawdy, bodacious, and beautiful. Like **The Grapes of Wrath**, this book became an instant bestseller. The reading public loved it.

However, many of the critics, as critics sometimes seem destined to do, harshly attacked it for being too rambling, too heavy-handed, too many obvious Biblical references. Some critics found it excessively violent with unnecessary sexual sadism. They claimed Cathy was overwritten, unbelievable, and far too brutal. Nevertheless, it was a runaway bestseller by November of 1952, right after its publication. Along with **The Grapes of Wrath**, about 50,000 copies of the novel are sold every year. In 2003 it was named Oprah's Book Club pick. Steinbeck considered it his finest work. In a letter to a friend, he wrote about the novel: "This is surely the most difficult work I have ever done. I have put all the things I have wanted to write all my life. This is the book. If it's not good, I have fooled myself all the time. Always I had this book waiting to be written." In 1955, the hit movie appeared starring James Dean and Julie Harris.

The novel does have some obvious flaws and structural challenges. The narrator is one of these challenges. It begins with a long first-person description of the Salinas Valley, told from the point of view of Steinbeck himself as a character in the novel, giving us the history of the story that is about to unfold. This first-person narrator then shifts to the third-person, providing observations, commentary, and side discussions about human nature, history, religion, philosophy, and economic conditions. And sometimes the narrator becomes one of the main characters, so the reader is challenged to pay attention. Adam Trask, Caleb Trask, Samuel Hamilton, and Cathy Ames all, at times, become narrators, and they, in turn, are sometimes interrupted by that first-person narrator making comments. This drove some literary critics crazy. I think it is ingenuous, powerful, and effective. Yes, one can easily get lost in this crazy-quilt narrative structure, but if you say alert, you are taken through an intricate series of stories and events from multiple points of view.

To manage all this is, I think, sheer writing mastery. Another structural challenge in the novel is that the Hamiltons, who are obviously very important to the book, only occupy about one-third of it. Yet, the moral voice of Samuel Hamilton is vital to the moral message of the novel. Although it is really a story about the Trask family, which includes Adam's wife, Cathy, the story of the Hamiltons provides a much-needed balance to the disturbing, dysfunctional Trasks, especially the violence and sadism of Cathy. On one level, the story is a kind of historical account of WWI and the Salinas Valley, with real people woven into the fabric of the story. On another level, it is a compelling, engaging, and very highly developed account of the personal lives of the key characters and their dramatic and often destructive interactions.

It is a complex series of plots and subplots, giving us an intricate tapestry, crafted with the full force of Steinbeck's creative genius. Manifest Destiny, creating a New Garden of Eden, and the American Dream are all intertwined in our national consciousness. Both **The Grapes of Wrath** and **East of Eden** hold up the hope of possibilities in the new land of California as the golden opportunity to realize the dream and create the new Garden. Head West, that's the mythic illusion. But Steinbeck, like F. Scott Fitzgerald, Hemingway, Faulkner, Theodore Dresser, Sinclair Lewis, Eugene O'Neill, Arthur Miller, Tennessee Williams, and many others, shows us all too glaringly that the American Dream can be a nightmare for many. The Garden of Eden is still seeped in evil, and the human capacity to discriminate, be unjust, and inhumane are far too prevalent.

We follow the lives of two families, the Trasks and the Hamiltons, and their interwoven and complicated stories. The Hamilton family is said to be loosely patterned after Steinbeck's maternal grandfather. We see the history of these two families from the beginning of the twentieth century through the end of WWI, though the novel also flashes back to the American Civil War period. The Salinas Valley itself serves as more than merely a backdrop. It takes on the importance of a character. The novel opens with a detailed description of this part of central California. Here are the opening lines of the novel:

> The Salinas Valley is in Northern California. It is a long narrow swale between two ranges of mountains, and the Salinas River winds and twists up the center until it falls at last into Monterey Bay.

> I remember my childhood names for grasses and secret flowers. I remember where a toad may live and what time the birds awaken in summer—and what trees and seasons smelled like—how people looked and walked and smelled even. The memory of odors is very rich.

We certainly sense Steinbeck's attraction to this area and his poetic power at capturing the beauty, wonder, and dynamics of it. That sets the stage for this powerful and deeply disturbing story. Immigrants from Ireland, Sam and Liza Hamilton begin the story. Kindhearted, hard-working, and decent folk, they raise nine children on a hard-scrabble farm. The children are growing up and gradually leaving the farm. In the meantime, Adam Trask purchases the best ranchland in the valley. We learn about his painful background and the brutal treatment he received from his half-brother Charles back on the farm in Connecticut. We meet Adam Trask's father, Cyrus, the Civil War veteran. We learn that Cyrus got rich by embezzling. We also learn about petty crimes Adam committed after his stay in the military. Adam eventually returns home where Charles, the brutal half-brother, tells him that his father left them each $50,000. Charles wonders if the money was earned legitimately.

We then meet Cathy Ames, who grows up in town not far from the Trask farm. We are told that Cathy has a "malformed soul." She is a master manipulator, delights in harming others, especially through deceit. One evening she sets fire to the family home, killing both of her parents, and leaves ending up as a mistress to a cruel man who manages prostitutes. He viciously beats her when he realizes she is using him, and he leaves her to die outside the home of Adam and Charles Trask. Charles sees Cathy for what she is, but naïve Adam falls in love with her and marries her. At the time of the wedding, Cathy seduces half brother Charles. She becomes pregnant with twins and the question remains—are they the sons of Adam or Charles? She fails at aborting them.

Adam takes his pregnant wife to California, settling in the Salinas Valley, having recently acquired wealth from his father. Cathy continually threatens to leave, so Adam locks her in the bedroom. When she finally talks him into opening the door, she shoots him and flees. Adam recovers but falls into a prolonged and deep depression. With the constant and devoted help of the Cantonese cook, Lee, and the neighbor Samuel Hamilton, they help Adam overcome his despair and help him name the two boys Aron and Caleb, names from the Bible clearly calling out the brutal story of Cain and Abel, which is retold in the novel.

You may remember the story. Briefly, Cain is the firstborn and Abel the second born of Adam and Eve after they are expelled from the Garden of Eden. Cain was a farmer; Abel a shepherd. They both made sacrifices to God, but God favored Abel's gift. Out of a fit of jealous rage, Cain murders Abel and flees. God's punishment of Abel is to send him to the Land of Nod, east of Eden, where he is forever a wanderer.

While Aron and Caleb are growing up, Adam, Lee, and Samuel have frequent and long discussions about the meaning of the Cain and Abel story as well as other philosophical debates about the Bible, morality, free will, and responsibility. Lee explains that a group of Chinese scholars spent years studying the Old Testament Bible and Hebrew beliefs. Lee points out that the Hebrew word "Timshel" means "Thou mayest." This is important in determining human motives and the roles of sin, guilt, and free will. The whole concept of a human's right and responsibility to choose is central to the novel. "Timshel" is the centerpiece of the novel. What each individual may or may not do and what each individual chooses to do has major moral consequences. The novel dramatizes the dialectical contest between good and evil. The Garden of Eden is lost. It has become corrupted. Much of Western history can be seen as an effort to recreate or rediscover or reestablish the Garden of Eden. The moral message of the novel is clear. You are free to choose good or evil. However, if you choose evil, there are grave consequences.

In the meantime, Cathy's story unfolds. She becomes a very popular prostitute in a brothel in the town of Salinas. She goes by the name of Kate Albey and embarks on an elaborate plan gradually to poison the madam of the brothel and take over herself. She is successful. The brothel becomes famous for its sexual sadism. Charles Trask dies but leaves money for Cathy who is now Kate. Adam goes to the brothel to give her the money. Kate scoffs at Adam, showing him pictures of the brothel's customers, many of whom are pillars of the community. Adam leaves feeling pity for Cathy/Kate, but she despises him.

Caleb and Aron grow up, unaware of their mother's situation. Aron is dutiful and virtuous and wants to become an Episcopal priest. Caleb is wild and rebellious and decides to become a farmer. Samuel Hamilton is now an old man and dies, mourned by the entire town. Adam starts a business that fails. Aron and Caleb are mortified by their father's financial failure. Caleb takes to wandering about town late at night, depressed and alone. He discovers that his mother is actually alive and running the brothel. He goes to see her. She is spiteful, telling him he is just like her.

Caleb, determined to earn back respect for his father's financial failure, goes into the business of selling locally grown beans to Europe at high prices during the war. He becomes very rich. He wraps up a gift of $15,000 for Adam, planning to give it to him that Thanksgiving.

Caleb gives Adam the money at dinner, expecting his father to be proud. Adam refuses to accept it telling Caleb to give it back to the poor farmers he exploited. Adam scolds Caleb with these penetrating words: "I would have been happy if you could have given me—well, what your brother has—pride in the thing he's doing, gladness in his progress. Money, even clean money, doesn't stack up with that." Of course, one of the ironies is that Aron was quitting his studies to be a priest, though Adam does not know this yet.

In a fit of anger and jealousy, Caleb takes Aron to see their mother, knowing he will be shocked. And indeed he is when he sees her. Consumed by self-hatred and despair, Kate signs over her estate to Aron and commits suicide. Aron goes off to the Army to fight in WWI. Another irony, he is killed in battle right at the end of the war. When Adam hears the news, he suffers a serious stroke. Caleb wins over Aron's girlfriend. She persuades Caleb to return home. The novel ends with Lee pleading with the bedridden and dying Adam to forgive Caleb. He does and then dies saying "Timshel." He frees Caleb to break the cycle of self-destruction.

Depravity, selfishness, greed, guilt, consequences for our actions, deceitfulness, and the human capacity to do harm are all played out in this powerful novel, packed with religious symbols and images. Clearly, this novel contributed to Steinbeck receiving the Nobel Prize for literature in 1962. In the final analysis, "Thou Mayest" choose to do good or evil is at the very heart of the book's moral message. The narrator makes this clear in the opening lines to Chapter 34, where he states:

> Humans are caught—in their lives, in their thoughts, in their hungers and ambitions, in their avarice and cruelty, and in their kindness and generosity too—in a net of *good and evil*. I think this is the only story we have and that it occurs on all levels of feeling and intelligence.

Steinbeck gives us a moving story of timeless themes. He probes the essential question of what it means to be human, what are our responsibilities to ourselves and to others and to our society. Where does such evil as displayed by Cathy come from? And yet she, too, struggles with her own choices. She is not amoral or unmoral. She IS immoral. And to be immoral, there must be a code of morality. Given the tension between good and evil, Steinbeck recognizes that evil exists in us all but that we also have the power of choice to do good. "Timshel!" as he wrote, "And now that you don't have to be perfect, you can be good."

If you have not read this novel or if you have read it some time ago, you are encouraged to read or re-read it, for it is packed with meaning and significance. The story of Cathy alone makes it worth our considered attention. There are, as you know, some incredibly memorable female characters throughout literature. Chaucer's Wife of Bath is one clear example. She stands out as a Medieval example of changing social mores, especially in terms of women. Shakespeare's Lady Macbeth is another famous female character, with her thirst for power and capacity for evil. Charlotte Bronte's Jane Eyre and Jane Austin's Emma are notable nineteenth-century women, as is Hawthorne's

Hester Prynne of **The Scarlet Letter** fame. And we all know Margaret Mitchell's infamous Scarlett O'Hara from **Gone with the Wind**. And we remember the seductive Maggie in Tennessee Williams's **Cat on a Hot Tin Roof**. There are many others. The point is that Cathy Ames, who becomes Kate, Trask and then Kate Albey, stands bold and firm among noteworthy female characters.

She is, to be sure, consummate evil. Steinbeck characterizes her as a "psychic monster" with a "malformed soul." This beautiful, cunning, attractive person has a strong sense of allurement. She's charming, seductive, and deceitful. There is a lot of snake imagery associated with her throughout the novel, suggesting Satan, expulsion from Eden, and complete depravity.

Remember, she manipulates and destroys people. As a young girl she frames two boys for attempted rape, she drives her Latin teacher to commit suicide, and she brags about her power to control people. She steals her own parents' money and then burns down their house while they are trapped inside, killing them. Before marrying Adam Trask, she drugs him and seduces his brother Charles. The unresolved question is: Who is the father of Caleb and Aron. While in California imprisoned by her husband Adam, she shoots him and flees, leaving the newborn baby boys to his care.

She then changes her name to Kate Albey and joins a whorehouse in Salinas, owned and managed by the kind Faye. She begins poisoning Faye while manipulating her to leave her the whorehouse. She finally gives Faye an overdose of pain medication, killing her. She converts the whorehouse to a popular den of sexual sadism and takes photographs of the patrons, which includes a local priest, politicians, business leaders, and others known in the community. Ironically, she does show some signs of remorse after she is discovered by both sons. She ends up giving all her possessions to Aron and then committing suicide by taking a lethal dose of morphine. Clearly, she is a dramatic illustration of the reality of Timshel and the living example of the dire, disturbing consequences of choosing evil.

In the 1955 film version of **East of Eden**, Jo Van Fleet won an Academy Award for Best Supporting Actress for her role as Cathy, and in the 1982 miniseries, Jane Seymour received the Best Actress Golden Globe Award for her portrayal of Cathy. In an interview with Oprah Winfrey, Ms. Seymour stated that "there is nothing greater than playing evil incarnate. It is wonderful. It is an amazing experience, because you climb into a spirit or a soul that you have no idea you know, you can't even imagine it." Steinbeck's literary genius is certainly on full display with his creation of this remarkable, albeit disturbing, character.

The National Steinbeck Center is a museum and memorial dedicated to him, located on the Main Street of Salinas, California, where he grew up and where so many of his major works are located. Founded in 1983, it was opened to the public in 1998. It is a magnificent structure that houses the largest collection of Steinbeck's archives, along with exhibits. It contains a theater, exhibition hall, a museum, and hosts many events throughout the year, including the annual Steinbeck Festival, the Steinbeck Young Author's Program, and many others.

Steinbeck frequently signed his correspondences and other works with his signature Pegasus logo. Pegasus, as you may recall, is a mythical, winged divine horse from Greek Mythology, symbolizing high-flying imagination. Usually shown as pure white, he is the offspring of the Olympian god Poseidon, and he is decapitated by another Greek god. Steinbeck's Pegasus logo is a flying pig and not a pure white horse. He explained that his Pegasus symbolized him as a "lumbering soul trying to fly." The Latin motto *Ad Astra Per Alia Porci* translates: "to the stars on the wings of a pig." Well, a touch of humor on Steinbeck's part and a fitting and interesting insight into his personality.

More importantly, this "flawed genius," as one critic describes him, gave us an enormous treasure of highly creative and powerful works of literature—some better than others. The body of the work is a magnificent testimony to his American Voice that still deserves to be heard. Ten years before his death, this conflicted soul wrote a letter to his son Thomas, who was only fourteen at the time and who had told his father he had fallen in love with a girl. The father writes this to his son:

> There are several kinds of love. One is a selfish, mean, grasping, egotistical thing which uses love for self-importance. This is the ugly and crippling kind. The other is an outpouring of everything good in you—of kindness and consideration and respect—not only the social respect of manners but the greater respect which is recognition of another person as unique and valuable. The first kind can make you sick and small and weak, but the second can release in you strength, and courage and good-

ness and even wisdom you didn't know you had…don't worry about los-
ing. If it is right, it happens—the main thing is not to hurry. Nothing
good gets away.

These tender words of advice, like the best of Steinbeck's writings, were
not hurried and were written from the right kind of love. And they are important, meaningful and powerful as a result, despite his many flaws and short-
comings. He also knew the wrong kind of love. He was not perfect. We want
our writers, pop singers, artists, and athletes to be representatives of the best
that human nature has to offer, saints or heroes perhaps, but that is unrealistic.
Like us, they, too, can be flawed. It is often important, even necessary, to separate the writer from the works created by that writer.

Steinbeck's career followed a rather typical pattern so prevalent in the
mid-twentieth century by so many artists. He struggles in the early years to
create a distinctive voice, to find an audience, and to gain recognition. He
achieves this by giving a powerful voice to the downtrodden. He enjoys a rapid
and amazing rise in fame and fortune. And then he declines into self-indul-
gence, crankiness, excessive drinking, and failed creative abilities.

We can list many other American writers that followed the same pattern,
such as: Hemingway, Eugene O'Neill, Tennessee Williams, and others. Nevertheless, Steinbeck discovered and developed his own distinct voice, an American voice to be sure, but unique, powerful, and moving. Part of the body of
his work stands as some of the very best testaments to the era of the Great Depression, followed by the booming post-war years. He gives us important insights into our own history, told through engaging, sensitive, and empathetic
stories of people who become real, who stand as representational of our country—its best and its very worst instincts.

We can return again and again to his important works and find ourselves
on the road with the Joads or on the ranch with the boy and his pony or struggling with Caleb and Aron. These memorable lines from **Cannery Row** capture his talent as he describes so poetically a typical day in the neighborhood:

> Cannery Row in Monterey in California is a poem, a stink, a grating noise,
> a quality of light, a tone, a habit, a nostalgia, a dream…. Its inhabitants
> are, as the man once said, 'whores, pimps, gamblers, and sons of bitches,'
> by which he meant Everybody. Had the man looked through another peep-

hole, he might have said, 'saints and angels and martyrs and holy men,' and he would have meant the same thing.

Yes indeed, the whores and the holy men comingle in Steinbeck's world as they do in the real world. His stories resonate. The people are real—trying to make it, struggling with their burdens, seeking dignity and respect and a small part of the American Dream. John Steinbeck is a gigantic American Voice. He gives us insights into the American spirit that is packed with passion, honesty, and empathy. He opens portholes into the very heart of the human soul, and for that he deserves our attention and gratitude.

THE MYTHIC AMERICAN WEST
And Its Writers

I confess that I must be a bit crazy to take on this topic. Like the West itself, it is so vast, so expansive, so difficult to contain and get your arms around. It is impossible to cover all aspects of the American West and its mythic dimensions in an essay such as this one. The intent is to present flavors, evoke memories, call for reflections, and encourage you to explore your own mythic West. We are going to ride roughshod over this big territory, looking briefly at several different landscapes and topics. Saddle up, hang on, and enjoy the ride.

When we think about the American West and ponder its significance in our history and culture, we are confronted by a complex series of dialectical clashes. It symbolizes regenerative power in the face of unimaginable destruction, the force of incredible opportunities in contrast to vast exploitation, a space that offers seemingly boundless hope and equally boundless despair, a place of both lost and found. What is your American West? When you think about the West, what images come to mind?

We know that myths and mythologies frame our consciousness and impact how we view ourselves, others, and our society. Virtually every society from every civilization has had its own mythologies. They serve as the emblems of those societies. They symbolize their beliefs, values, customs, and traditions. Myths and mythologies have two diametrically opposed significances. On the one hand, they formalize constructs of the legends, folktales, and stories that were passed down from generation to generation. Many if these myths are crossovers from earlier traditions. For example, many Christian traditions, such as Easter and Christmas, have roots in primitive traditions and customs. On the other hand, myths and mythologies can easily and quickly become romanticized, sentimentalized, and distorted stereotypes of their original intentions. This process alters substantially these intentions, which, as we will see, can lead to exploitation, abuse, prejudice, and even destruction.

The West means vastly different things to different peoples. The Native Americans' view of the West is diametrically opposite, on many levels, to that of a white rancher. Such differences apply as well to Latinos, African Americans, and even subgroups within ethnic populations. Certainly, myth is an integral part of the West, just as it is and has been for all cultures and societies. Before the Europeans came to North America, it has been estimated that there were over 500 distinct Indigenous societies (white settlers called them tribes and Columbus misnamed them Indians) with their own languages and with multiple mythic stories about creation, life and death, the past and the future, and their distinct human hopes and fears.

For the American Indian, nature was a sacred part of their mythic stories and nature sat at the center of their universe. Nature was to be revered, for it is the giver and sustainer of all of life. Traditionally, Indigenous Peoples felt rooted in their place in the world, with a strong sense of belonging and identity. To remove them from their place destroys their sense of identity. The myth that allowed that to take place so aggressively and so successfully is one clear example of the destructiveness such a myth had and continues to have on Native Americans. This harsh reality will be developed further on in this essay.

Let me explain that I use the terms Indian and Native American and Indigenous People interchangeably, recognizing that there is ongoing debate about what is the most appropriate name to use. The fact that Columbus misnamed them has not effectively changed that title. When I was a professor at a college in Montana, I also served as the faculty advisor to the Indian students at the college. We had discussions about the "politically correct" or preferred or most appropriate title to use, and the majority of these students, as well as their parents and the tribal elders, referred to themselves as Indian and assured me that it was fine for me to use that name as well. We know that in Canada Indigenous populations are referred to as First Nation Peoples, and in Mexico they are referred to as Indigenous Peoples of Mexico or Native Mexicans.

The legends and stories among the differing North American Native nations that were passed down from generation to generation are a long-lasting tradition. Of course, a continued concern is that these stories, like their languages, are and have been rapidly fading. There are efforts to preserve these stories and languages. Many have already been lost. Once gone, the culture, traditions, customs go as well. A lost past all too easily becomes a forgotten people. That is part of the sad story of Native American Peoples. We know that to understand the present and to anticipate effectively the future, it is helpful, perhaps necessary, to know the past. Nevertheless, we are blessed in our country to still have significant Native mythologies and traditions. The concept of the Great Spirit, the notion that spiritual forces are embedded in nature, the symbolic significance of animals, such as the eagle and the bear, these mythic threads can still be found and appreciated in Native ceremonies, celebrations, artworks, and literature.

Whatever has survived from Indian legends, stories, mythologies, and customs has been overshadowed and overpowered by a dominant white exploitation of both the land and the Native Peoples. There is no shortage of examples of a Mythic West defined and perpetuated by non-Indians, even including fabricated images of what the Indian was or should be. Here are some prominent and popular examples that built an elaborate quilt of myths about the West and its peoples, be it Indian, cowboy, miner, or marshal.

This fictional former Texas Ranger fights for justice and apprehends outlaws with his trusty Indian sidekick, Tonto, on their beautiful and well-trained horses, Silver and Scout. Like many of our Western TV series, it began back in 1933 as a radio show and a series of **Long Ranger** books. It ran for eight seasons from 1949–1957 on TV, starring Clayton Moore and Jay Silverheels. **Bonanza** aired on television from 1959–1973—fourteen seasons, the second longest running TV western series behind **Gunsmoke.** Set in the 1860s on the Cartwright ranch in Nevada, Lorne Greene played Ben Cartwright, the father, Pernell Roberts played Adam, Dan Blocker was Hoss, and Michael Landon was Little Joe.

Gunsmoke, the longest running western TV series, lasted from 1955–1975, with 635 episodes. It covers the escapades of Marshal Matt Dillon, starring James Arness, and his trusty sidekick Ken Curtis as Festus, along with the cranky Doc Adams and Miss Kitty Russell. She runs the saloon in Dodge City, Kansas. In love with Matt, she can't quite get him to take off his gun belt or his boots, not to mention his pants.

Based on the best-selling novel by Larry McMurtry, published in 1985, did anyone not watch all or some of the TV series **Lonesome Dove**? This epic adventure was seen by an estimated 26 million homes from 1989–1990. **Longmire** and **Yellowstone** are two more recent examples of TV series that mythologize the West, and both are exceedingly popular.

These, and so many others like them, create a complex series of beliefs, concepts, and images about how the West was settled and by whom. The histories that play out the expansion westward are linked to the Frontier and all the facts and fictions related to our understanding of how this Frontier was shaped.

The Frontier Myth of the West is central to our American history and culture. What is meant by the Frontier shifts as westward expansion pushes the boundaries farther and farther outward, beginning with the Colonies, then to the Ohio River, then to the Mississippi and finally to Texas, California, and the Pacific Northwest, with all the other Western Territories in between. The importance of the Lewis and Clark Expedition (1804–1806) is certainly critical in opening the doors to this unknown area. Its mission was to explore territory all the way to the Pacific, to establish peaceful trade with the Natives, and to affirm the sovereignty of the United States over these lands.

Although mainly set in the deep woods of the New York region, James Fenimore Cooper is not only considered the first noteworthy American novelist, but his **Leatherstocking Tales** are also viewed as "Frontier Novels." Natty Bumppo is patterned after the legendary Daniel Boone.

The five novels in this series focus on the major events in Bumppo's life from 1740–1806, and they depict the French and Indian Wars, life among the Natives, settling the wilderness, and explorations to new territories. Cooper sets the stage for what we now call Western novels.

Before we cross the Mississippi heading westward, we move from the deep, dark woods and rugged Allegheny Mountains of Leatherstocking to the banks of the Ohio River, our next Frontier. At the Peace Treaty in Paris in 1783, John Adams and John Jay insisted that all the lands controlled by the British west of the Allegheny, northwest of the Ohio River and east of the Mississippi become part of the United States. This became known as the Northwest Territory and eventually became the States of Ohio, Indiana, Illinois, Michigan, Wisconsin, and Minnesota. This huge track of unexplored land was referred to as "the new frontier," with only a few forts, no real settlements, and mainly trappers, traders, and explorers living among the Natives. They often married Native women. For an outstanding historical analysis of the Northwest Territory expansion and the life of those who settled this region, see David McCullough's very interesting book, **The Pioneers: The Heroic Story of the Settlers Who brought the American Ideal West** (2019). David McCullough, a Pulitzer Prize and National Book Award winner, died on August 7, 2022 at the age of eighty-nine. This American historian gave us many excellent studies that help us understand the past.

With the ceding of the Northwest Territory to the United States, one of the most important developments that continued westward exploration and expansion and the entire concept of Manifest Destiny was the Northwest Ordinance. This significant development came to be considered "The American Way of Life." The Northwest Ordinance stipulated that there would be freedom of religion throughout the region (for whites, that is), education was to be a priority in the settling of the lands, there would be no slavery, and a new State was to be established, which became known as Ohio.

The white settlers' frontier myth was based on the concept that at the edge of civilization lay vast regions open for expansion and exploration and that it is the American right to settle these regions. It was a God-given mandate manifested by the American Dream. The determination of these self-reliant people was to create a new life—never mind that this frontier was already inhabited by significant Native populations. This myth was actually a theory developed and practiced by political and religious leaders, educators, farmers, the military, and business entrepreneurs. Frederick Jackson Turner's Frontier Thesis was written in 1893, titled "The Significance of the Frontier in American History," which he presented at the American Historical Association conference in Chicago during the Chicago World's Fair. Of course, the belief in white superiority and the right to take over the land was central to western expansion long before Turner articulated his theory.

Turner defined the concept of the frontier as "the meeting point between savagery and civilization," and he argued that "the very foundation of our iden-

tity as a country and our politics and policies are shaped by this very concept."
American expansion, Turner continues, is the westward movement in waves,
which pushes the frontier outward and makes way for civilization. As the fron-
tiers are settled, the nation is being transformed. Nationalism, democracy, and
individualism, according to Turner, become the new cornerstones of the country. European customs and ideals are being replaced by this emerging frontier
spirit. Turner concluded that it is precisely the concept of the frontier that
makes America unique. More than merely an abstract, academic thesis,
Turner's concepts of the Frontier becomes embedded in the very myths about
that Frontier.

This concept of the Frontier, which is reinforced and amplified by Manifest Destiny and the American Dream, meant that any obstacles, be they
Native Americans, African Americans, or Mexicans, could be removed or eliminated if necessary. It was out of this concept that many of our national heroes
emerged, such as Daniel Boone, Davy Crocket, Buffalo Bill Cody, Annie Oat-
ley, followed by the iconic cowboy. This white western hero became an arche-
type in our mythology depicted in the literature, movies, television, and comic
books as an essential part of Western folklore. This folklore produced such
popular shows as **The Lone Ranger, Gunsmoke**, and **Have Gun Will
Travel**. John Wayne and a whole gang of colorful, engaging characters become
emblematic of this Frontier myth. They are rugged individualists, who love
their freedom, carry a strong sense of justice, wear white cowboy hats, and
sing "Happy Trails to You" and "Home, Home on the Range."

As an aside, I had the distinct honor and privilege of working with Roy
Rogers and his son Dusty on a feature-length video, titled **Man the Hunter**.
Roy and Dusty narrated this video, and we also used old footage from some of
Roy's Alaskan hunts. We spent several days in September of 1990 filming the
fiftieth anniversary of the One Shot Antelope Hunt. The tradition began in
1940 as a contest between Colorado and Wyoming as to who had the best
hunters. Over time, it evolved into a very large event bringing together many
celebrities. I wrote the script for this video. Roy Rogers and his son were exceedingly kind, thoughtful, decent people, and it was a joy to work with them.

These western myths are very powerful and very difficult to demythologize. The belief, for example, that the frontier cowboys were brave, generous,
unselfish men prevails, along with the notion that the West was won by noble

soldiers and pioneers fighting brutal, scalping savages, is still prevalent today. There is, of course, another more accurate side to this depiction. The American Dream has its own nightmares when we look openly and honestly at our history. How the West has been spun is being recast in a more accurate and less mythic manner.

For example, the white-hatted hero with a quick draw and true shot in the name of justice really did not win the West. That legend may make for exciting movies, TV series, or novels, but the reality is that the West attracted a lot of marginal drifters with the promise of land and riches. Many were immigrants and many were down-and-outers, as well as criminals. The early cattle towns, like Dodge City, were violent places where the likes of the Dalton Gang, Jesse James, and Billy the Kid rode roughshod over justice. John Wayne stands as a strong representation of this self-reliant knight. He starred in over eighty western movies, showing the towering cowboy as a heroic, laconic, stranger riding across the prairie to save a maiden from the savage Indians. Although the cowboy stands as one of the dominant and endearing myths about the West, in reality, he was typically lonely, malnourished, underpaid, and drifted from ranch to ranch seeking work. The blue-eyed American boy, with James Dean features, was more often Mexican, half-breed, or African American.

Nevertheless, this legendary cowboy remains a deeply embedded emblem in our consciousness. All you have to do is travel some summer to Cody, Wyoming and watch the hokey re-enactment of a blazing shootout outside the Irma Hotel, which Buffalo Bill Cody had built and named for his wife, or attend the Cody rodeo to witness how strong the legend continues. One important dimension of this legend is that the cowboy, as a rugged individualist, represents a central concept in American history and culture. That concept places the value and importance of the individual above all else. That concept is supported and enhanced by Manifest Destiny and the American Dream. The history of our country may be seen as a conflict between individualism as a God-given right versus the larger well-being of society.

In most other cultures, such as Native American, African, Japanese, Chinese, and many others, the good of the whole, that is, what's best for the community and all of society, is valued above the importance of the individual. We see this conflict played out over and over again. Indeed, one reason the cowboy stands so tall as a heroic monument is precisely because he represents the enduring value of the individual. This is both a blessing and a curse. The ongoing political debate over gun rights is a classic illustration of this conflict. Wearing or not wearing a protective mask or getting or not getting the COVID vaccine during the recent pandemic are also strong indicators of how deep this conflict is within our country.

Another long-standing mythic concept is tied to the land and the rights of ownership, which is ingrained deeply within the powerful rights of the individual. The Homestead Act of 1862 offered up to 160 acres to any American white person as long as a structure was erected on that land and it was worked. This promise of free land led to a huge migration westward from the East. Although the land was free, so were the many wildfires, the infestation of pests, dust storms, and soul-crushing loneliness. Read Laura Ingalls Wilder's **Little House on the Prairie** (1935), which was also a popular TV series that romanticized pioneer life, and Willa Cather's **O Pioneers** (1913) to get a vivid sense of the harsh realities of homesteading. The romanticized concept that traveling West in a wagon train was a happy family adventure was hardly reality.

Remember the popular TV series, **Wagon Train**? Ronald Reagan, Lee Marvin, Bette Davis, and others all made guest appearances on the show. It was directed by John Ford, who produced many popular Western movies. These wagon train excursions were brutally harsh, very dangerous, and often resulted in death. But the lure of the land had strong appeal. And the rights of the individual was embedded in the right to own property, even to take it away from those who previously inhabited that land. The concept of owning land was foreign to Native Americans. For someone to claim such ownership and then to put fences around it was contrary to their customs, beliefs, and traditions.

The thrill of instant wealth by finding gold is yet another myth of the West. When gold was discovered in 1848 in California, thousands flooded to the hills in pursuit of the elusive glitter. Within two months, a reported 4,000 people were prospecting in the foothills of the Sierra Nevada. A few did strike it rich. They fostered tall tales of grizzled men buying rounds of drinks in a ramshackle bar in some makeshift town, where men outnumbered women by ten to one. In the span of five years, the California Gold Rush yielded approximately 16 billion dollars in today's money. Actually, the lone prospector all too often became an underpaid worker living and working in dangerous conditions. Racial conflicts were common in mining towns as prejudice against the Chinese, Indians, Blacks, and Mexicans prevailed.

With the burgeoning population of men rushing to these mining camps and towns, the lure of wealth also enticed madams to set up brothels. The proverbial myth of the prostitute with a heart of gold is another illusion easily debunked. Read Steinbeck's **East of Eden**, for his portrayal of Kate, the prostitute and madam, describes vividly the harsh realities of this life. The fable that the prostitute treated her customers fairly, gave anonymously to the local church, and eventually married a rich rancher is clearly debunked in Anne M. Butler's book, **Daughters of Joy, Sisters of Misery** (1985), an excellent account of what life was like for those women making a living off the sexual pleasures of men.

Nevertheless, these mythic dimensions are the very stuff on which the enormously popular and still-thriving American literature known as the Western novel are made, a genre that has its roots in The Leatherstocking Tales. When I use the term Western novels and Western novelists, I recognize that there are many excellent writers and novels that are about the West but do not fit into this specialized category. John Steinbeck, for example, sets his magnificent novels mainly in California, but he is not considered a Western writer. If you were to Google the Best Western novels, you would see several lists of the top fifty, top twenty, or even top ten greatest Western novels.

What is this Western novel genre? Fundamentally, these novels give us a nineteenth or twentieth century medieval knight in new armor as the all-conquering hero, the valiant warlord, the ancient wanderer, and the undaunted fighter—all decked out in cowboy boots, hat, and riding a magnificent steed. What's so unique and so very American is that the Western hero is basically a common man—me and you, drawn into the necessary business of saving the fair woman in distress and catching the bad guy. His roots are ordinary—not aristocratic, not highly educated, not from blue-blood ancestry. He is the Romanticized Self, the strong-willed individual.

Geographically, the Western novel is typically set west of the Mississippi River, usually in Texas, New Mexico, Colorado, Wyoming, and Montana. These novels are peopled with cowboys, ranchers, homesteaders, sheriffs, marshals, gunfighters, gamblers, and lovely, lonely women. Strong landscapes and strong characters are the hallmarks of these novels, along with a writer who can weave a damn good tale, packed with adventure and usually ending with justice preserved and the wrong righted. These writers entertain us and shape our concept of the West. For an excellent discussion of the myth of the cowboy and the winning of the West, see the essay by Karen Jones, "How the Wild West was Spun," **BBC History Magazine**, 2014, or "How the West was Spun," by Annie Proulx, **The Guardian**, 2005. Many of the points I make about the mythic cowboy are adapted and borrowed from these essays.

Any discussion of the Western novel should begin with the great Zane Grey, a prolific writer of more than ninety books. He was also a practicing dentist. Although most of his books are Western novels, he also wrote histories, fishing, and adventure books, hunting stories, children and travel books. Over 100 films have been made as adaptations of his books, as well as three TV series. He became the first millionaire novelist in the US. His Western novels reached the top of the bestsellers' list nine times in his lifetime. It is generally accepted that Grey's **Riders of the Purple Sage** is his best work. The novel is packed with romance and adventure, and still stands today as a classic Western novel.

Louis L'Amour's **Hondo** was his first full-length novel and is regarded as one of his very best Western novels. Hondo is your strong, silent type with the classic themes of man against nature, man against himself, and man against his enemies. Like Zane Grey, L'Amour also wrote histories, essays, short stories, science fiction, poetry, and nonfiction, though he is best known for his Western novels, many of which were made into movies. He died in 1988 at the age of eighty. Also, like Zane Grey, he was a prolific writer, with over 100 published works of which eighty-nine were novels. He received the Presidential Medal of Freedom and Congressional Gold Medal.

Any serious consideration of the Western novel should include Owen Wister's **The Virginian**, which was also a long-running TV series. A. B. Guthrie is simply a masterful story-teller, who captures the West during the Rocky Mountain fur trading boom of 1820–1850. He brings us back to the West before roads, the loss of the bison, and the conquered Indian. **The Big Sky** series features mountain men, who are obsessed with their independence. Guthrie is the real deal.

Norman Maclean, who wrote the best-selling **A River Runs Through It**, which, for my money, ranks as one of the very best modern Western novels. The movie, starring a young Brad Pitt and produced by Robert Redford, came out in 1992, sixteen years after the novel. It was a big hit. The novella and movie, **Legends of the Fall**, were both enormously popular. The book was written by Jim Harrison, and the movie also starred Brad Pitt, along with Anthony Hopkins and other top actors.

The late, great Tony Hillerman creates a subgenre within the board category of Western Literature. A captivating murder mystery writer, he set his novels on or around the Navajo Indian reservation and creates the memorable characters of Joe Leaphorn and Jim Chee, who are Tribal Police Officers. A recent TV series, titled **Dark Winds**, produced by Robert Redford, brings his popular stories to the screen as a captivating depiction of contemporary Navajo life and intriguing crime stories woven into that life. His daughter, Anne Hillerman, carries on this tradition. At present, she has seven novels in the series that continue the original series of her father, and her eighth is scheduled to come out next year. C. J. Box is another Western novelist that mainly writes murder mystery novels featuring the iconic Joe Pickett as a Wyoming Game Warden. Continuing this tradition is Craig Johnson with his Walt Longmire series. Box and Johnson give us good reads and capture the flavor of Wyoming with its vast landscape, majestic mountains, and colorful characters.

Larry McMurtry is arguably one of our greatest Western writers. His compelling power to capture places and people and to weave them into masterful stories are a testament to his creative abilities. He is a treasure. Nostalgic for the old Texas, McMurtry's novels are steeped in the West Texas lore of the romantic cowboy on the range. From his early novel made into the movie **Hud**, to **The Last Picture Show,** or **Terms of Endearment,** or **Lonesome Dove**, he seeks to capture the "cowboy sensibility," no matter how sentimental that sensibility appears. To be sure, he recognizes that the landscape can be dark and bloody, but that cowboy character remains a strong voice of human survival and independence.

One of my very favorite Western novelists is the Montana-born and raised Ivan Doig, who died in 2015. He writes of immigrant families, dedicated schoolteachers, fur trappers, bartenders, and the engaging Rocky Mountain area, where his characters face the uncertainties of love, the threat of nature, and the struggles to survive. His last novel, **Last Bus to Wisdom** (2015), is a marvelous, funny, witty coming-of-age story that ends up on a ranch in Wisdom, Montana, after a zany, touching bus journey from Wisconsin to Montana. The description of the annual Crow Fair in the novel is spot-on.

Thomas McGuane and Cormac McCarthy are also both worth reading. Each in their own dramatic and creative manner brings us face-to-face with the West and its people and landscape. Although not restricted by the Western novel genre, McCarthy's **All the Pretty Horses**, which won the National Book Award, and **No Country for Old Men** are both vivid depictions of the West.

There are so many others, such a vast and engaging array of talent. The West clearly inspires some of our very best writers. There is something about the big skies, magnificent mountains, expansive prairies, the storms, the places, the people, the high drama—all of it capturing the imaginations and giving creative inspiration to so many talented writers. And I have not even talked about cowboy poetry, which is also a big part of the Western Literary Tradition. Of course, we shouldn't ignore either Country & Western Music. We could spend an entire essay on this alone. The pony express, the laying of the railroad tracks, the development of towns and cities, the important roles of Hispanic, Chinese, and Blacks, and so much more—unfortunately, we don't have time to cover all of these important aspects of western history and mythology.

The Mexican-American War is another glaring example of the power of Manifest Destiny. It costs the lives of approximately 25,000 Mexicans and 13,000 Americans. It was plainly and simply a land grab in which the US Government took a huge chunk of property from Mexico in order to expand the slave-holding States. However, a far more costly, protracted, and deadly military engagement by the US Government became known as the American Indian Wars, which lasted intermittently from the Colonial Period until the end of the nineteenth century. During this time, there were countless treaties made and broken, many full-scale military operations against the Indians, numerous massacres, forced marches for relocation, and a whole series of laws allowing for white Americans to settle on Indian lands.

It is very difficult to determine accurately the total number of deaths of the US soldiers, the white settlers, or the Indians. Records were not often kept and those that were kept were not very accurate. For a shocking idea of the toll in lives and taken land, Google these three documents: "List of Indian Massacres," "American Indian Wars," "Trail of Tears," and also see "How

Many Native Americans were Killed by the US Government," which comes from the Native American History of the US and found on the internet. Much of the facts, statistics, and information presented in this essay dealing with these issues come from these articles.

In an effort to try to give some realistic assessment of the toll on Native Americans, there are reasonable estimates that Indian populations across North American prior to the British Colonies ran between 15–20 million people, and some project much higher numbers. However, the 1890 US Census estimated that there were fewer than 200,000 Indians alive in the US. To state this from a different perspective, Native American Nations occupied over 2.4 billion acres of land in the US prior to European settlements. By 1900, Indians controlled only about 3% of US land, most of which was designated reservations. For a useful, intensive, and engaging discussion of population trends, broken treaties, and taken lands, see David Treuer's **The Heartbeat of Wounded Knee: Native America from 1890 to the Present** (2019). Treuer, a member of the Ojibwe Tribe from the Leech Lake Reservation in northern Minnesota, brings together carefully researched history, memoirs, and astute observations of Indian life in this important book. I borrow from it in this essay.

Realistically, the decimation of Native Americans is clearly our country's terrible holocaust. This conscious and systematic genocide occurred over three centuries and happened through a combination of efforts that include smallpox and other diseases, massacres, forced relocations, and military engagements. Conservatively, over 14½ million native peoples died as a direct result of these acts of extermination. On a brighter note, the 2010 US Census records over 2 million American Indians, with more than 70% living in urban areas. While Manifest Destiny was great for many Europeans settlers who went West, it was a death knell for Native Americans. Slavery and the treatment of the Native Americans are telling indicators of systemic and lasting racism. This racism remains a heavy, dark, and troubling hole in our national soul. We see that this hole is far from healed today. We are capable of healing it, I hope and believe, for it must be healed if we are truly to be a diverse and inclusive Democracy that lives up to the promise of our Bill of Rights, Civil Rights, and American Ideals.

One of the critical events that shaped this mass destruction of our Native

Peoples was, of course, Custer's Last Stand or Battle of the Little Bighorn, when Ulysses S. Grant was President. This battle was unique for several reasons. First of all, it brought together several tribes that historically and traditionally were enemies—the Lakota Sioux, the Cheyenne, and the Arapaho. It took place on traditional Crow Indian lands along the Little Bighorn River (an area I fished many times). The Crows scouted for the US Calvary. There is some strong evidence to suggest that these Crow scouts knew about the pending battle and the location of the large Indian army of over 2,000 warriors, led by Chief Crazy Horse against Custer's force of around 700 men. By the way, this battle is re-enacted every year on the Crow Reservation, and the Crows play the roles of the attacking Indians. I participated in this re-enactment twice back in the 1970s. After the Indian victory over Custer, retaliation came in many forms. One of the most glaring and disturbing was Wounded Knee, under President Benjamin Harrison. At Wounded Knee, an estimated 300 Indians were slaughtered, and they were mostly women, children, and old men.

The Trail or more accurately TRAILS of Tears is yet another glaring reminder of man's ability to perform heinous acts of cruelty against fellow human beings. These brutally forced marches took place primarily from 1830, with the passage of the Indian Removal Act, through 1838. Andrew Jackson was president, and US Congressman Davy Crockett of Tennessee vehemently opposed the act itself and the suffering and deaths caused by these forced marches. By 1838, over 46,000 Indians from the southeastern states had been removed from their homelands, opening up 25 million acres for white settlements.

One of the most horrific of these marches was the removal of the Cherokee peoples from east of the Mississippi and as far as Florida forcing them during the winter to march over 1,000 miles to Oklahoma, resulting in approximately 4,000 deaths—some put the death toll as high at 8,000. These various forced relocations impacted and decimated over ten separate tribes, with total deaths well over 15,000 Native peoples.

A number of very important books have been published over the past fifty years that play an important role in demythologizing white man's histories about the Natives. To mention a few that deserve our attention: **Custer Died for Your Sins**, Vine Deloria, Jr. (1969), **Bury my Heart at Wounded Knee**, Dee Brown (1970), **Blood and Thunder**, Hampton Sides (2006). These are still very relevant historical studies helping us demythologize the past.

To present a much more hopeful aspect of the resilience of our Native brothers and sisters, art among Indian peoples is exploding. Scott Momaday's Pulitzer Prize winning novel, **House Made of Dawn** (1968), stands as a great read. Louise Erdrich, another very popular Native author, is often on the best-seller list. She is an important voice in the Native American Renaissance movement of artists. Her novel **The Plaque of the Doves** (2008) is outstanding. A more recent novel by Tommy Orange, **There There** (2018), has generated a lot of positive attention and is well worth reading. The poet Joy Harjo is certainly an important Native American voice well deserving of our attention. She served as the Poet Laureate of the United States from 2019–2022, has published several volumes of poetry, and has edited the very valuable treasure, **When the Light of the World was Subdued, Our Songs came Through: A Norton Anthology of Native Nations Poetry** (2020). There are many, many other examples.

Toward the end of his insightful, though at times very disturbing book, **The Heartbeat of Wounded Knee**, David Treuer points out a number of reassuring facts. Some of them are: 32% of present-day Indians are under the age of eighteen compared with 24% in the overall US population; between 1990–2000, American Indian income increased by 33% and the poverty rate dropped by 7%; the number of Indian-owned businesses and Indians being elected to state and local governments continues to grow at very encouraging rates; and the number of Natives attending college has doubled in the past thirty years. Treuer writes: "the net effect of all this diversity (the demographic and economic changes) is a sense that we are surging…. No longer does being Indian mean being helplessly characterized as savage throwbacks living in squalor on the margins of society…." He further states that he feels Indians are using opportunities in the best possible way: "to work together and to heal what was broken." He goes on to ask all Americans this important question: "What kind of a country do we want to be?"

To remember and retell the important stories of the past, Treuer maintains as part of the answer to this question, not only about Indians but about all who suffered injustices, racism, discrimination, and abuses of power, for that helps us understand our past in order not to replay it over and over again. Those stories should remind us, Treuer continues, "to remain humble in power, and to be called to tend to the troubled soul of the country; it is to remember that our very lives exist at the far side of policy. It is to remember the good and the bad, the personal and the social, the large and the small. It is not to capture Indians, per se, but to capture the details of our lives. We are, for better or worse, the body of our republic. And we need to listen to it, to hear—beyond the pain and anger and fear, beyond the decrees and policies and the eddying of public sentiments and resentments, beyond the bombast and rhetoric—the sound (faint at times, stronger at others) of a heartbeat going on." That is how he ends the book.

Part of my goal is this far-ranging and rambling essay is to present to you the diverse heartbeats of the West and to suggest that these heartbeats give us long-lasting and memorable messages. The literature, movies, music, and art reveal the mysteries, magic, and the magnificence of this space. The power and sustainability of these heartbeats are testimony to the West itself. It is the perfect place to house, foster, feed, and cherish our diversity because it is so majestic. There is a Native American symbol of a bird in flight leaving its circle, entitled "Giving Flight to Life." This symbol, like the classic Phoenix Bird who is reborn from its own ashes, represents the powerful re-emergence of Native cultures. It also radiates potentials, possibilities, hopes and dreams, and the resilience of the human spirit, regardless of origins, languages, or skin colors. The West calls us beyond the myths, past the despairs, and beckons us to cherish the value of our diverse heartbeats. I hope my goal was achieved.

THE MYTHIC WEST & ITS WRITERS

Works & Authors Referenced In The Essay

{Listed in order presented}

James Fenimore Cooper, 1791–1851 – **The Leatherstocking Tales: The Pioneers; The Last of the Mohicans; The Pathfinder; The Prairie; The Deerslayer**

David McCullough – **The Pioneers** (2019)

Laura Ingalls Wilder, 1867–1957 – **Little House on the Prairie**

Willa Cather, 1873–1947 – **O Pioneers**

John Steinbeck, 1902–1968 – **East of Eden**

Anne B. Butler – **Daughters of Joy, Sisters of Misery: Prostitution in the American West, 1865–1890.**

Karen Jones – "How the Wild West was Spun," **BBC History Magazine,** 2014

Annie Proulx – "How the West was Spun," **The Guardian,** 2005

Zane Grey, 1872–1939 – **Riders of the Purple Sage**

Louis L'Amour, 1908–1988 – **Hondo**

Owen Wister, 1860–1938 – **The Virginian**

A. B. Guthrie, 1901–1991 – **The Big Sky Series**

Norman Maclean, 1902–1990 – **A River Runs Through It**

Jim Harrison, 1937–2016 – **Legends of the Fall**

Tony Hillerman, 1925–2008 – **The Fallen Man,**

(**Dark Winds** is a new TV series based on Hillerman's novels)

Ann Hillerman – **The Tale Teller**

C. J. Box – **Wolf Pack; Out of Range**

Craig Johnson – **Land of Wolves**

Larry McMurtry, 1936–2021 – **Hud; The Last Picture Show; Terms of Endearment; Lonesome Dove**

Ivan Doig, 1939–2015 – **Last Bus to Wisdom**

Thomas McGuane – **The Missouri Breaks**

Cormac McCarthy – **All the Pretty Horses; No Country for Old Men**

David Treuer – **The Heartbeat of Wounded Knee**

Vine Deloria, 1933–2005 – **Custer Died for Your Sins**

Dee Brown, 1908–2002 – **Bury My Heart At Wounded Knee**

Hampton Sides – **Blood and Thunder**

Scott Momaday – **House Made of Dawn**

Louise Erdrich – **The Plaque of the Doves**

Tommy Orange – **There There**

Joy Harjo – **An American Sunrise, When the Light of the World was Subdued, Our Songs Came Through: A Norton Anthology of Native Poetry**

THE PROPHETIC VISION OF GEORGE ORWELL AND HIS POLITICS OF POWER
Animal Farm and 1984 Revisited

"…that man does not live by bread alone,
that hatred is not enough, that a world worth
living in cannot be founded on 'realism' and machine-guns."
Orwell, "Notes on the Way"

"Totalitarianism has abolished freedom of thought to
an extent unheard of in any previous age."
Orwell, "Literature and Totalitarianism"

"GOD IS POWER" Winston Smith, *1984*

"The Prophetic Vision of George Orwell" is centered in his potent, insightful, and disturbing depictions of how power corrupts. His voice sent strong and honest warnings throughout England, Europe, and the US during the 1930s and 1940s. These warnings are still very relevant for us today. His voice is still very much alive. This essay is also titled: "The Politics of Power." Virtually all of Orwell's writings, which include essays, memoirs, novels, and criticism, have to do with power politics—how power threatens freedom, destroys community, erodes human dignity, and exploits others for its own end. This essay explains both Orwell's prophetic voice and his concern with the abuses of power. To illustrate both the relevance of his message and his concerns about corrupt power, we will look at his last two novels, which are also his best, **Animal Farm** and **1984**.

I wrote my doctoral dissertation on George Orwell, titled **Politics in Orwell's Fiction**, which was completed in 1973. It studies the political development of Orwell from his first novel, **Burmese Days**, published in 1934, to his last, **1984**, published in 1949. Along with E. M. Forester's **Passage to India**, written ten years earlier and surely known by Orwell, **Burmese Days** is an important study of the politics of imperialism. Orwell well understood firsthand that colonial control of one country by another leads to exploitation, racism, and a condescending erosion of that country's culture and history. He also understood that the controlling country pays a heavy price itself. As Orwell wrote in a famous essay about his experience as a police officer in Burma when he was beckoned by the villagers to shoot an elephant that had gone mad: "I perceived in this moment [he has just shot the elephant with a crowd of natives jeering him on] that when the white man turns tyrant it is his own freedom that he destroys" (see "Shooting an Elephant," by George Orwell). These are powerful and prophetic lines. Orwell came to recognize that the imperialistic exploitation of one country over another means that the tyrant is tyrannized by his own tyranny. Of course, the ultimate expression of this reaches full horror in **1984**, Orwell's last novel.

Orwell wrote six novels. The first is **Burmese Days**, followed a year later by **A Clergyman's Daughter**, 1935. This novel explores the exploitation of organized religion. It is a flawed but delightful novel about a young girl, whose father is an Anglican priest. We see her coming of age in a highly political institution, the Church of England, and her subsequent disillusionment and loss of faith.

Orwell's third novel was published in 1936, entitled **Keep the Aspidistra Flying**. This is a novel about rebellion, Orwell's version of an artist as a young man, and his mounting alienation with English middle-class life. The aspidistra plant symbolizes the hollowness of that life. Orwell's fourth novel, published in 1939, is **Coming Up for Air**, and it is a powerful depiction of the politics of modernism. This prophetic novel predicts the coming of WWII, the decay of modern civilization, and the growth in Russia and Germany of totalitarianism. **Coming Up for Air** describes the hollowness of a culture being torn apart by political, social, and cultural divides, specifically the dehumanization caused by industrialization.

The political development of Orwell in these four novels, as well as the other books and many essays he wrote from the early 1930s until his final work in 1949, show a clear and steady maturity to his brilliant and culminating last two novels, **Animal Farm** and **1984**. These last two novels are still relevant, for they are loud cries of warnings over seventy-five years later. Orwell's life and some of his other writings help us better understand the development of his prophetic voice and his passionate concerns about authoritarianism.

In the past few years, interest in Orwell's books and life have seen a remarkable and understandable resurgence. No doubt, the contentious, highly charged political atmosphere in the US and elsewhere have kindled this renewed interest. **Animal Farm** and **1984** have enjoyed renewed popularity, new books and essays about Orwell have appeared, Broadway played a dramatic adaptation of **1984**, the movies based on **Animal Farm** and **1984** have been playing the theaters, and some of Orwell's favorite expressions, like "Big Brother is Watching You," "War Is Peace," "Freedom Is Slavery," and "Ignorance Is Strength" have re-emerged in our popular culture on hats, T-shirts, and bumper stickers. A fairly recent book about Orwell was published in 2017 by Pulitzer Prize winning author Thomas Ricks, titled **Churchill & Orwell: The Fight for Freedom**. Ricks points out that although both men never met, they both spent their entire lives fighting against oppression and for freedom. It is no accident that Orwell names the main character in **1984** Winston. Churchill is reported to have read the novel more than once and that he raved about it.

Orwell's relevance is also illustrated by the ongoing efforts to ban **Animal Farm** and **1984** from our high school and public libraries. These self-appointed, self-righteous, zealously pious "protectors" of our moral consciousness remain threatened by the force of Orwell's voice. Their solution is to attempt to silence his voice, along with the voices of many others we should heed.

Orwell matters today as much as he did in the 1930s and 1940s because his prophetic voice fiercely fought against the twin towers of totalitarianism—Communism and Fascism, as did Churchill. Orwell understood that the key challenge facing the twentieth century at that time and into the future was not, as Karl Marx wrongly asserted, who controls the means of production, but rather who controls the political systems that either thwart or promote freedom. Orwell has a lasting impact on us today because he spent his entire life promoting liberty and attacking forces that seek to control or destroy freedom. As he states: "If liberty means anything at all, it means the right to tell people what they do not want to hear." This means for Orwell writing the truth and presenting the facts as he saw and understood them.

Throughout all his many essays, articles, reviews, nonfiction books, and novels, the most important theme running loudly and clearly in his life and his writings is his concern for the perversion of power. Orwell explores how power corrupts, the ramifications of such corruption, and the costs in lost freedom and human sacrifice as a result of such misuses of power. Orwell always sides with the underdog, the poor, the working class, the exploited, the disenfranchised, and the down-and-outers. His perspective is that those in positions of authority and power over others, be it institutionalized religion, political parties, Dickensian school masters, power-hungry police, military leaders, or heads of government, always work to preserve their power by obscuring the truth, victimizing others, instilling fear, spreading rumors, and changing history in order to maintain this control. The king, Orwell well understood, does not willingly give up the throne—neither does Hitler or Stalin.

It is very important to remember that during the 1930s and 1940s in England and throughout Europe, as well as the US, two very life-threatening, world-changing events were taking place. The first was the Great Depression. The second was the mounting evidence that Germany was on the march and that another world war was in the making. The mood was gloomy. A popular belief of those times was that the end of Western civilization was at hand. There was a consensus that the experiment of capitalism as an economic system was done. The new ideology of Karl Marx and Communism was appealing to many intellectuals and working-class people, including those in the US. T. S. Eliot, Ezra Pound, James Joyce, and a host of other writers, as well as historians, philosophers, and other intellectuals depicted a world on the brink of decay and destruction. There was a malaise, a sense of doom, a despondency.

WWI was to be the end of all wars, but all too quickly there were strong signs that WWII was going to happen. The social, political, and cultural context during the 1930s left a huge hole, and the false and artificial promises of Communism, on the one hand, and Fascism, on the other, filled the void. In 1939, the great historian Arnold Toynbee gave a lecture at the London

School of Economics, entitled "The Downfall of Civilizations." In 1938, Neville Chamberlain, the Prime Minister of England, and Adolf Hitler reached the famous Munich Agreement in which England agreed to appeasement toward Germany. There was strong support in the US and Europe, including England, to look the other way, to acquiesce to Hitler, and to remain isolated. Remember, it took the bombing of Pearl Harbor, years after the war had started, before the US entered the war. When it finally did, there was still strong and loud opposition. These are important lessons in history—lessons Orwell does not want us to forget.

Some very startling but telling examples to illustrate this historical context happened on May 14, 1938. Remember, WWII began September 1, 1939. The British soccer team played Germany before a crowd of over 100,000 people in Germany. During the playing of the German National Anthem, both teams gave the Nazi salute. That same spring, Lord Halifax, head of the British Foreign Office, told Czechoslovakia that it should make concessions to Hitler. Ironically and shockingly, on September 29 of 1938, Prime Minister Chamberlain flew to Berlin to make a deal with Hitler. He returned to London and announced that he had "secured peace for our time." He was greeted by cheering crowds in the streets of London. WWII started one year later. Orwell had written and spoken frequently about the threats of both Fascism and Communism long before the war began. These examples should remind us of the dangers democracy faces today, for there are strong and concerning movements to weaken and destroy democracies.

It is important to understand that for Orwell, politics penetrates virtually every aspect of life. Although not every human activity is overtly political, politics shapes individual attitudes, values, actions, and determines our social structures and institutions. Like the great novelist Charles Dickens, Orwell is best described as a "moral revolutionary." He understood the complex difficulty of improving the world. He also realized that there is a fundamental tension between those who wish to improve human nature by changing the very institutions that shape this nature and those who wish to improve these institutions by changing human nature. Orwell took a strong stand somewhere in between these two alternatives. His politics are firmly rooted in his passionate belief in equality, justice, and freedom, all essential to democracy. He opposes any form of ideology or doctrine that threatens these.

Orwell based his hope for democratic freedom on a very clear concept of patriotism. As he maintains in one of his many political essays, patriotism is "the bridge between the future and the past." This bridge represents a joining of two sides in Orwell that are often in conflict with each other and which creates a great deal of tension in his novels. One of these two sides is his strong faith in the English tradition, a tradition he found in Chaucer, Shakespeare, Milton, Blake, and Dickens. The other side is his equally strong faith in the possibilities for democratic socialism as essential for a hopeful future.

It is important to distinguish Orwell's support for patriotism from the rampant nationalism that was being fostered in Germany. We see strong support for such nationalism re-emerging today both in the United States and in other countries, with frightening echoes of Fascism. Orwell detested nationalism, which promotes the belief in the superiority of one country or one race over others. For Orwell, one can be very patriotic, love one's country, support the customs and traditions of one's culture, but still not believe that one's country or a particular race has the right to control, exploit, invade, dominant, or colonize another country or have authority over other races. He loved England but bitterly opposed its oppressive control of India and Burma (now Myanmar).

Born in India on June 25, 1903, Eric Blair (George Orwell becomes his pen name) died at forty-six on January 21, 1950. Though he died way too young, he lived a very eventful life. Famous for his lucid, clear, and insightful prose style, he was a school teacher, shop owner, worked in a bookstore, fought in the Spanish Civil War, served in the British Home Front in London, was a cultural and political commentator for the British Broadcasting Company, served as a police officer in Burma, lived among the poor and homeless, studied poverty, exposed the exploitation of miners in northern England, and raised beautiful roses. He was married twice. His first wife died during surgery in 1945, and his second wife he married right at the end of his life. He had one child, a boy he had adopted. In addition to the six novels he published, he also wrote three autobiographical memoirs, four large volumes of essays, and numerous letters.

Graduated from Eaton College, he joined the Indian Imperial Police in Burma in 1922 and served there until 1927. His experiences in Burma gave him essential materials for his novel, **Burmese Days**. He also wrote some essays and stories about his life there, including one that is well known, named "Shooting an Elephant." He moved to Paris in 1928, working at odd jobs and paying close attention to poor people there, as well as in London, where he returned to live after nearly two years in Paris. His astute observations are captured in his important study of poverty, homelessness, and those disenfranchised by society, **Down and Out in Paris and London**, published in 1933. It remains an insightful study of the exploitation of the poor. Much more than simply an intelligent, insightful, and empathetic account of the life of down-and-outers, Orwell's own political views are shaped by what he observed. This is the first book in which he uses his pen name and he uses it for all his other publications.

Besides **Down and Out in Paris and London**, he published two other important autobiographical books or memoirs as personal accounts of his own experiences and observations. All three are still very readable and relevant today. His second nonfiction book continues with his concern for human dignity in the face of class discrimination and exploitation. **The Road to Wigan Pier** was finished and sent to his publisher in 1937, four years after **Down and Out in Paris and London**. His first two novels, **Burmese Days** and **A Clergyman's Daughter** had already been published, and they, along with these two books, gained him recognition as a serious writer. In January of 1936, Orwell went to the coal mining region of Wigan, in northern England. Living among the coal miners and witnessing firsthand their lives and the life-threatening conditions of the mines, Orwell's book becomes a penetrating and disturbing exposé of social injustices and the horrible lives of the coal miners. This landmark work led him to be placed under investigation and surveillance by a branch of the British government for twelve years—one year before he publishes **1984**.

In December of 1936, with four books now completed, Orwell's voice was being heard and his works read. He sets out for Spain to fight in the Spanish Civil War in order, as he states, to combat Fascism and defend democracy. He joined a rag-tag group of underfed, poorly equipped, and untrained revolutionaries. Although supposedly supported by the Russian Communists, Orwell soon discovers that the war is a mass of lies, distortions, and contradictions. He realizes that Russia, as was Germany, was supporting both sides selling arms and supplies to Franco and to the rebels. This confirms his serious disillusionment with Communism and increases his strong opposition to Fascism.

While on the front lines in Spain, he is shot through the throat by a sniper, which takes him out of combat and lands him at a sanatorium in Barcelona. This wound caused him serious medical issues the rest of his life. His very important and still very readable book about the Spanish Civil War, **Homage to Catalonia**, was published in 1938. As a member of the Workers' Party group of soldiers, which he joined purely by chance and not out of any allegiance to Communism, Orwell was charged in Spain with treason. After all, the revolutionaries lost. The Fascist government of Franco was victorious and was supported by Germany. Orwell's book created quite a stir in England, for many of the intellectuals supported Communism. His strong attacks against both Communism and Fascism put him out of favor with the English Left.

Smell—the stench of dying, the decay in the trenches, the odor of bad food, and the foul smells from dirty uniforms—plays an ongoing role in this book. Here is a line from the book that is so typically Orwellian: "We were near the front line now, near enough to smell the characteristic smell of war—in my experience the smell of excrement and decaying food." Smell is also very prevalent in **Down and Out in Paris and London** and it also plays a very strong role in **1984**.

His experiences, misadventures, and wound in Spain brought Orwell to the disillusioned reality that blind allegiance to a cause may be disingenuous and downright dishonest. As he writes, "You had all the while the hateful feeling that someone hitherto your friend might be denouncing you to the secret police." And indeed that happened frequently. At a time when solidarity to Communism was considered mandatory if you were truly a leftist, Orwell came to realize that the Communist Party in Europe and England, controlled by Russia, betrayed the revolution in Spain.

His account in the book of being badly wounded by a bullet is one of the best accounts ever written of what it is like to be wounded and close to death. Orwell fled Spain in June of 1937. He realized that he was lucky to get out alive. Many of his fellow soldiers and friends did not. They were hunted down and executed. The book makes it crystal clear that both the rightwing movement of Fascism and leftwing movement of Communism were equally packed with lies. He saw firsthand the corruption of power politics. He left Spain resolved to spend the rest of his life vigorously fighting the abuses of power.

Orwell's warnings of this clash between Communism and Fascism proved correct, for on August 23, 1939, Germany signed a nonaggression agreement with Russia. As Orwell maintained, with that agreement, the totalitarian right made a pact with the totalitarian left. For Orwell this was an alarming moment of clarity. The misuses of power on both ends of the political spectrum were clearly evident. On September 1, 1939, he reports that "blackberries are ripening in the countryside of England and the finches are beginning to flock together," but the invasion of Poland has begun, he laments. WWII was starting.

By August of the next year, 1940, it is clear that Germany intends to bomb England, and heavy bombardments filled the English skies all that summer and on into the fall of that year. Indeed, the bombing of London begins in late August. You might recall that Ambassador Joseph Kennedy urged England to surrender. The US was still hoping to stay out of the conflict, and there was strong sentiment in the US to remain neutral.

Orwell tried to enlist in the army but was rejected because of his wound in Spain. He joined the Home Front to help his fellow Londoners cope with the bombings. He wrote no novels during these troubling war years from 1939 until 1943, when he began work on **Animal Farm**. However, he did produce many essays, articles, and other works of journalism during this time. Many of his essays described the horrible impact the bombings had on the people of London. On June 22, 1941, Germany violates its Nazi-Soviet Pact and attacks Russia. As we all know, on December 7, 1941, the Japanese attack Pearl Harbor, which brings the US into the war.

With the surrender of Germany on May 8, 1945, Orwell's view of the world was indeed very bleak. He was not alone. Many other writers, political leaders, and intellectuals viewed the world through a very dark lens. The political influence of Russia under Stalin's rule, along with Stalin's ability to dictate how the world was to be divided up, gave Orwell and others cause for serious alarm. The freedom that was fought for in this brutal war, many feared, was giving way to an emerging totalitarianism that sought to destroy freedom. His most important works, **Animal Farm** and **1984**, emerge from this fear.

In May of 1946, two years after the publication of **Animal Farm**, Orwell goes to live on a remote island in Scotland, where he begins writing his penultimate work, **1984**. While on the island, he has a boating accident that nearly costs him his life. Already suffering from acute tuberculosis and advised by doctors to live in a warmer climate, Orwell's health is rapidly deteriorating. He finished writing **1984** in December of 1948 and has it published to widespread acclaim in June of 1949. He had left the island that January and went to a sanatorium in England. He married Sonia Brownell on October 13, 1949, with her promise to take care of his son and his financial affairs. On the morning of January 21, 1950, he died at the age of forty-six. He is buried at the Anglican Church in Oxfordshire.

Orwell subtitled **Animal Farm** "A Fairy Story." Although he means this ironically and satirically, he is tapping into a long tradition of fables featuring talking animals that represent people. This tradition is well known in Europe and popular throughout England, going back to ancient times with Aesop's Fables. Rudyard Kipling's **The Jungle Book** was very popular at the end of the nineteenth century, the height of the British Empire. In 1902, the popular **The Tale of Peter Rabbit** appeared—the year between the death of Queen Victoria and the birth of Orwell. It sold millions of copies. Virtually every British youth would be familiar with the Peter Rabbit series. In the 1920s A. A. Milne's **Winnie-the-Pooh** and his animal friends also were very popular. And there were other popular animal fables.

Orwell frames the book as a fairy tale and uses animals as the main characters. This gives him the latitude and creative freedom he needed to write this powerful attack on political control, violence, and the exploitation of power. It begins with utopian optimism but soon turns into a nightmare of totalitarian control. Set in rural England on a typical farm, the real landscape is the Russian Revolution and the violent battle for power between Trotsky and Stalin.

Animal Farm appeared in bookstores in England five months after his first wife's unexpected death during surgery and three days after the end of WWII. The original 5,000 copies printed sold out within the first two months, and it has not stopped selling and being read since its publication. It still stands today as one of the most important books ever written in the English language and perhaps of all times and all languages.

Because Orwell's last two books are fictionalized analyses of the nightmare of totalitarianism, it is important to understand what Orwell means by totalitarianism. There is a significant body of scholarly studies on totalitarianism. One of the best is Hannah Arendt's **The Origins of Totalitarianism**, published in 1951. Eric Fromm's book, **Escape from Freedom**, published in 1969, is another important study. Basically, totalitarianism goes beyond the corrupt power of a dictatorship and demands, indeed enforces, complete subservience to the state. The state has absolute and unlimited authority and seeks to regulate every aspect of public and private life. In his essay, "Literature and Totalitarianism," Orwell writes that "There are several vital differences between totalitarianism and all other orthodoxies of the past, either in Europe or in the East." He goes on to state that traditional orthodoxies did not, for the most part, tell you to believe one thing on Monday and another on Tuesday. He concludes that "with totalitarianism, exactly the opposite is true."

Animal Farm, while written in simple prose, like Hemingway's **The Old Man and the Sea**, and while it is shrouded in this animal fable, is a harsh indictment of how easily power can become total, that the corruption of power can quickly become all-encompassing, and that the process is insidious in its ability to gain such complete control. Whereas Farmer Jones controlled the physical actions of the animals, the pigs control completely language, thought, and actions. By the end of the story, Napoleon's rule is so complete that it is impossible for the animals to determine whether or not they were better off under the harsh meanness of Farmer Jones or now after the revolution. As Orwell writes in the novel, the animals "could not remember. There was nothing with which they could compare their present lives: they had nothing to go upon except Squealer's lists of figures, which invariably demonstrated that everything was getting better and better." Of course, we know that the animals are far worse off under Napoleon's control than they were under Farmer Jones's.

In the final scene of the book, the pigs are playing cards and drinking with the humans with whom they do business. Napoleon and one of the humans are both cheating. The other farm animals are watching through the window. And the novel concludes with this all-telling irony: "The creatures outside looked from pig to man, and from man to pig, and from pig to man again; but already it was impossible to say which was which." The totality of the authoritarian control is complete. Despite the hope of a better life after the revolution, **Animal Farm** dramatically demonstrates that the energy of corruption gains a terrifying momentum that cannot be stopped. The logic of domination takes on its own force and fury. Much more than an overt satire on Soviet politics, Orwell presents a direct warning that totalitarianism can and does easily and swiftly occur, especially if ordinary people give up their own political power to stop it.

In his final novel, **1984**, that warning becomes louder and more frightening. Orwell shifts from an animal fable to a futuristic horror story in the tradition of such dystopian works as Huxley's **Brave New World**, Anthony Burgess's **A Clockwork Orange**, and more recently, **Klara and the Sun** by Kazuo Ishiguro (2021). Published in June of 1949, the same month that Winston Churchill's second volume of **Their Finest Hour** came out, Orwell would die less than seven months later.

With shades of T. S. Eliot's **The Wasteland**, which opens with "April is the cruelest month," **1984** begins with: "It was a bright cold day in April, and the clocks were striking thirteen." Thus, the reader is launched into a world gone astray. He goes on to describe the smells of the dwelling where Winston Smith resides: "The hallway smelt of boiled cabbage and old rag mats." Winston, the anti-hero, passes a poster with the caption all in bold, capitalized words: **BIG BROTHER IS WATCHING YOU!**

We are invited into a time in the future in which objective reality does not exist and any attempt to establish truth, with a capital "T," is illegal by the State. There is universal surveillance conducted by the Thought Police, using telescreens. Even the children are rewarded for spying on their parents. You are being watched, the narrator tells us, all the time. Foreseeing today's omnipresent electronic capabilities, with Facebook, Twitter, and governments' abilities to gather information on its citizens, Orwell raises the essential question of freedom, privacy, and individual rights. As Winston gazes out the window of his seedy apartment, he sees the looming Ministry of Truth building with the three slogans of the Party:

WAR IS PEACE
FREEDOM IS SLAVERY
IGNORANCE IS STRENGTH

Ironically, of course, the frightening realities are that the Ministry of Peace is actually engaged in war, the Ministry of Plenty ensures poverty and shortages of food and clothing, and the Ministry of Love invades the privacy of peoples' lives so that even sex is controlled. In this alarming context, Winston begins his own private revolution. He writes in his diary: "Down with Big Brother." He realizes that the Party insists that people reject as truth what they see with their own eyes. His effort to find truth and reject the totalitarian world begins. He adds to his diary: "Freedom is the freedom to say that two plus two makes four. If that is granted, all else follows." Again ironically, Winston and Orwell are tapping into the philosophical foundations of bygone English intellectuals, like John Locke, David Hume, and John Stuart Mill, all who developed theories about empirical truth, individual freedom, and the limits of government control. The State in **1984**, of course, denies any empirical truth. There can be no objective reality in a totalitarian state.

The book is packed with ironies. One of the most important is that Winston's job is with the Ministry of Truth as a historian, whose responsibilities are to rewrite history, to create "Fake News," as it were. As Winston observes, "If the Party could thrust its hand into the past and say of this or that event, it never happened—that, surely, was more terrifying than mere torture and death." Of course, he will soon find out that torture is far more terrifying. The woman in the cubicle next to him has the job of deleting all records from the past, so that people who were eliminated never even existed. This, as we know, actually happened in Germany, Russia, and elsewhere. Winston works on a machine called "Speakwrite," a name that foreshadows software programs of the future. At the edge of his desk is the "memory hole," where historical documents disappear as though truth does not matter.

One of the central themes in the book, which is carried throughout all of his novels and reiterated in many of his essays and nonfiction books, is a faith in the working class, the proletarians. As Winston reflects in his diary, "If there is hope, it lies in the proles." Of course, the control by the State ensures that the working class are kept oppressed and distracted by the sheer weight of poverty and forced labor they must face to survive. The small, personal revolution Winston carries on reaches its full and ironic climax with his sexual relationship with Julia. They begin their affair in the countryside. For these doomed lovers, sex is the ultimate form of rebellion. As the narrator tells us, "Their embrace had been a battle, the climax a victory. It was a blow against the Party. It was a political act."

Of course, their little rebellion is violently squashed by the State. While in prison, both Winston and Julia are broken by torture and forced to not only confess but to blame the other person. As Winston's torturer, O'Brien, asserts: "You believe reality is something objective, eternal, existing in its own right. You also believe that the nature of reality is self-evident.... But I tell you, Winston, that reality is not external.... Whatever the Party holds to be truth _is_ truth. It is impossible to see reality except by looking through the eyes of the Party." Both Julia and Winston are forced to accept this grim reality. The horror of complete control is complete; it is total. The novel ends with the two broken lovers confessing to each other their respective betrayals, and then they part. No hope is offered in the novel.

As a thirty-nine-year-old functionary in the Outer Party of Insoc, Winston Smith is responsible for committing one of the worst sins a person can commit. He falsifies and alters history. Not only does he participate in this heinous activity, he does it well. The narrator of the novel tells us that "Winston's greatest pleasure in life is his work." We come to understand that Winston is a schizophrenic. In fact, Orwell writes in one of his essays that "Totalitarianism, however, does not so much promise an age of faith as an age of schizophrenia." Throughout the novel, we see Winston struggling with his own identity. Through his affair with Julia, he tries to establish the fact that he is actually alive. However, over and over again, the novel exhibits that these people, including Julia and Winston, are walking dead; only the proles have some semblance of being alive. The final defeat of Winston occurs when he commits his ultimate sin against humanity. O'Brien breaks him through his vicious torture, and Winston cries: "Do it to Julia! Do it to Julia! Not me! Julia! I don't care what you do to her. Tear her face off, strip her to the bones. Not me! Julia! Not me!"

Although Orwell illustrates Winston's failure as a human being in the face of a perverse, destructive, and totally controlling system, we are still meant to feel some compassion, some empathy, some understanding toward him. It would be too easy to condemn him outright. That misses the power of the novel. In important and effective ways, we are drawn to him with a profound sense of loss, sadness, and horror. Afterall, he is, as is Julia and the others in the novel, suffering from acute loneliness. That is the paralysis of totalitarianism. The novel's brilliance makes that reality powerfully real.

The ultimate hope for the prevention of totalitarianism exists outside the context of **1984**. Those who are tyrannized by the power brokers of Orwell's world in 1949 have the capacity to prevent totalitarianism from gaining control before it is too late. By the time we meet Winston Smith in that future year of "1984," it is already too late. Orwell makes that forcefully clear. By focusing on the future as he does in the novel, he makes his most dramatic and creative case for the present and for our future against totalitarianism.

Throughout Orwell's writings, the importance of community and his faith in the common person are central tenets of his belief in democracy. In his essay, "Looking Back on the Spanish War," written in 1942, Orwell recalls seeing an enemy, who "jumped out of the trench and ran along the top of the parapet in full view. He was half-dressed and was holding up his trousers with both hands as he ran." Orwell confesses that he "refrained from shooting at him. It is true that I am a poor shot and unlikely to hit a running man at a hundred yards, and also that I was thinking chiefly about getting back to our trench while the Fascists had their attention fixed on the aeroplanes. Still, I did not shoot partly because of that detail about the trousers." And in one of the most telling political statements Orwell makes about himself, he writes: "I had come here to shoot at 'Fascists;' but a man who is holding up his trousers isn't a 'Fascist,' he is visibly a fellow creature, similar to yourself, and you don't feel like shooting at him."

Orwell's refusal to shoot the "enemy" is consistent with his humanitarian politics. He believed that politics should be rooted in values, in moral principles, in a fundamental civil sense of decency. In all six of his novels, liberation is an illusion and tyranny is the reality. He seeks to penetrate the mask of illusion and expose the grim truth of modern society. Orwell sees that society suffocates the average person. From **Burmese Days** to **1984**, Orwell marks our development toward new methods of control, which are frightening, sophisticated, terrifying methods. Nevertheless, there is also the belief that we can achieve the liberating hope of liberty, justice, freedom, and democracy. What hope exists within his six novels actually rests with the readers themselves. Orwell's analysis implies that there is a need to create a new order, a new politics. The responsibility to establish this new order rests with those of us who are impacted by the sheer force of his analysis.

Language, Orwell understood, controls us. As he wrote in his important essay, "Politics and the English Language," "if thought corrupts language, language can also corrupt thought." He understood that the corruption of language facilitates the corruption of politics and vice versa. This corruption allows those in power to commit heinous acts against humanity without facing moral consequences. Despite the horror he so effectively presents in his novels, Orwell's faith in the capacity of people to be decent and humane underlies the horror and calls for us to be morally responsible. His prophetic voice shouts loudly and forcefully against hatred, racism, and corrupt power. He reminds us that our freedom, liberty, and dignity are in our hands, for we have the power to effect change and to protect and cherish these essential tenets of life. **Animal Farm** and **1984** are both prophetic and powerful warnings. They deserve our concerned attention.

About the Author

Robert Van Dellen earned his Ph. D. from Indiana University, taught literature at a college in Montana, went into business for more than twenty years, and returned to academia at a college in Michigan where he ended his career as the campus president. Along the way, he taught undergraduate and graduate-level courses, both on-line and on-ground, conducted numerous seminars and training programs for non-profit and for-profit organizations, and has delivered many talks on literature and other topics. He enjoys playing golf and pickle ball, has been an avid backpacker and wilderness canoeist, and is a lifelong student of literature. He and his wife live on a lake in northern Michigan during warmer months and in Florida during the winter. They delight in travel, especially to visit families and their nine grandchildren. You are invited to visit his website at: www.BobTalks.Me

Reflections On Literature:
Exploring Meanings And Messages

Robert Van Dellen, Ph. D.

A FIVE-VOLUME SERIES OF ESSAYS THAT WILL BE AVAILABLE
AS COMPLETED & PUBLISHED

Volume I: The Modern Novel from the Roaring Twenties to the Mythic West—-completed
- Introduction
- Searching For the Lost Generation: Literature During the Roaring Twenties
- Hemingway's Key West and Cuba——The Old Man and The Sea
- A Literary Giant: The Life and Works of John Steinbeck
- The Mythic American West and Its Writers
- The Prophetic Vision of George Orwell and The Politics of Power: Animal Farm and 1984 Revisited

Volume II: Touching Our Souls: The Significance of Poetry
- Introduction
- Why The Caged Bird Sings: The Amazing Voices of Maya Angelou and Her Legacy
- Making Connections: The Visionary Poetry of Mary Oliver
- Two Great American Poetic Voices: Walt Whitman and Robert Frost
- William Blake's Creative Genius: Painter, Poet, Prophet
- Poetic Gems: Great Poems and Their Meaning—-From Shakespeare to T.S. Eliot & Beyond

Volume III: Dramatic Encounters: Four Great Playwrights
- Introduction
- Eugene O'Neill: A Great American Playwright
- Tennessee Williams: Another Great American Playwright
- The Tragic Vision of Arthur Miller
- Shakespeare's Wondrous World: His Tragic and Comic Visions

Volume IV: <u>Life's Lessons from Literature: Friendship, Love, and Death. Huck Finn, King Lear, Moby Dick, Thoreau, Pat Conroy, and Others</u>
- Introduction
- Friendships In Literature: The Blessings and The Curses
- Who Doesn't Love a Good Love Story
- Growing Up and Facing Death Through Literature
- Pat Conroy: From the Pain of Suffering to the Glory of Forgiveness

Volume V: <u>Literary Wanderings—-Journeys and Destinations from Impressionism to Louise Penny, From Thoreau to Five Nature Writers</u>
- Introduction
- Wandering Through the Landscape of Impressionism in Art and Literature
- The Novels of Louise Penny: High Tea with Chief Inspector Gamache and the Characters of Three Pines
- The Urgent Relevance of Henry David Thoreau's Prophetic Voice
- Odes to Earth: Lessons from Five of Our Best Nature Writers (Dillard, Bass, Williams, Lopez & McKibben)

For more Information, see: www.BobTalks.Me

CPSIA information can be obtained
at www.ICGtesting.com
Printed in the USA
LVHW052356030723
750310LV00002B/9